MAURICE RAVEL

Gaspard de la nuit

for Solo Piano

Edited by / Édition de / Herausgegeben von
Roger Nichols

Urtext

EIGENTUM DES VERLEGERS · ALLE RECHTE VORBEHALTEN
ALL RIGHTS RESERVED

PETERS EDITION LTD

A member of the EDITION PETERS GROUP
FRANKFURT/M. · LEIPZIG · LONDON · NEW YORK

Peters Edition Limited
2–6 Baches Street
London
N1 6DN
England

Tel: +44 (0)20 7553 4000
Fax: +44 (0)20 7490 4921
e-mail: sales@editionpeters.com
Internet: www.editionpeters.com

© Copyright 1991 by Peters Edition Limited, London

All rights reserved. No part of this publication may be reproduced, stored in a retrieval system or transmitted in any form or by any means, electronic, mechanical, photocopying, recording or otherwise, without the prior written permission of the publisher.

CONTENTS

Ravel's Piano Music – A New Edition

Editorial Method and Sources v

Preface vi

Principes d'édition et sources vii

Préface ix

Editorische Methode und Quellen x

Vorwort xii

Gaspard de la nuit

I: Ondine 1

II: Le gibet 14

III: Scarbo 19

Critical Commentary 39

RAVEL'S PIANO MUSIC – A NEW EDITION
Editorial Method and Sources

There is no denying the excitement of holding in one's hand the autograph manuscript of a musical masterpiece; and where the autograph is itself a work of art, as many of Ravel's are, then aesthetic considerations also come into play to compound the excitement. But there is equally no denying that composers are, like all mortals, fallible, and that however beautiful and exciting an autograph is, it may nonetheless contain mistakes. The apparently laudable desire to go back to what the composer originally wrote needs therefore to be tempered with a certain amount of common sense.

With stage works, it is true, pressures of time, space, money and personalities often lead to deformations which the composer does not in any sense welcome but has to accept if the performance is to go ahead, and which may then find their way into the printed score. But in the case of piano works, the pressures on the composer in preparing an edition are much slighter, exerted for the most part by the printer in his desire for conformity with house style, so that changes introduced between manuscript and edition have a somewhat greater chance of representing decisions freely taken by the composer. Certainly, in the process of publication mistakes may be introduced as well as rectified and, when musicality and common sense indicate that this may have happened, the autograph can indeed sometimes provide vital evidence. But in the course of conversations with a number of composers of our own time, I am given overwhelmingly to understand that they would actually be angry if future editors ignored their carefully prepared printed scores and went back automatically to their original autographs for a so-called true reading.

In the case of Ravel's piano music, such a critical view of autograph evidence is more than ever justified, since the Music Department of the Bibliothèque nationale de France holds a bound volume containing Ravel's own printed copies, with autograph corrections, of the bulk of the first editions of his solo piano music.[1] To judge from the contents, the volume would appear to have been made up between 1911 and 1913. The works missing from this collection are *Sérénade grotesque*, *Sites auriculaires*, *Ma mère l'oye*, *Prélude*, *A la manière de...*, *Le tombeau de Couperin* and *Frontispice*. Printed copies with autograph corrections of *Ma mère l'oye* and *A la manière de...* are held separately in the same institution,[2] while Ravel's own printed copy of *Le tombeau de Couperin*, with autograph fingerings and one autograph correction, is on display in the Musée Ravel at Montfort l'Amaury. For *Sérénade grotesque* and *Sites auriculaires* the autographs may be said to assume paramount importance since these pieces were not published in the composer's lifetime. The autograph of *Frontispice* is also significant because Ravel's own printed copy has not been found. Unfortunately, for *Prélude* neither the autograph nor the composer's printed copy is extant.

No proofs are known to survive of the first editions of any of Ravel's piano works, apart from a set of first proofs of *Le tombeau de Couperin* in the Durand archives, marked up by the Durand editor with a request for second proofs (I am grateful to Roy Howat for providing me with a copy of this material). This set contains no autograph markings. All the editorial annotations found their way into the first edition except for the form of some of the multiple appoggiaturas in 'Prélude' and 'Forlane' of *Le tombeau de Couperin*, over which Ravel would seem to have changed his mind.

Primary Sources

Where Ravel's own corrected edition is available, I have taken it as my main primary source; discrepancies between this corrected edition (**CE**), the first printed edition (**E**) and the autograph are duly noted. The autograph of *Valses nobles* (nine pages in the Taverne collection) has not itself been made available for study, but a microfilm (**AM**) is held in the Music Department of the Bibliothèque nationale de France (Vm. micr. 876).

Secondary Sources

The secondary sources fall into four groups:

(a) Printed copies with corrections by musicians close to Ravel

(i) Copies of Ravel's piano music belonging to Robert Casadesus (**CasCE**), now also housed in the Music Department of the BnF; his copy of *Valses nobles* is shelved as Vm. Casadesus 940. It contains no markings in the composer's hand.

(ii) Some copies, including that of *Valses nobles*, belonging to Vlado Perlemuter (**PerCE**), also now housed in the BnF, but awaiting cataloguing.

(iii) Some copies with corrections by Lucien Garban. Garban worked for the Durand publishing house and was a close friend of the composer. The exact status of these corrections is impossible to determine but, given the links between the two men, it is feasible that at least some of the changes were dictated by Ravel. These copies are now in the library of Bakersfield College, California. Garban also made piano duet transcriptions of *Valses nobles et sentimentales* and *Le tombeau de Couperin*. These are published by Durand.

(iv) Copies not consulted include those belonging to Jacques Février, whose niece and pupil Mme Aboulker-Rosenfeld has assured me that they contain no markings beyond his fingerings; and those of Henriette Faure, which cannot be located.

(b) Ravel's own orchestrations of a number of his piano pieces (**RO**). In chronological order of original composition (dates of orchestration in brackets), these are: *Menuet antique* (1929), 'Habanera' from *Sites auriculaires* (1908), *Pavane pour une Infante défunte* (1910), 'Une barque sur l'océan' and 'Alborada del gracioso' from *Miroirs* (1906 and 1923), *Ma mère l'oye* (1911), *Valses nobles et sentimentales* (1912), 'Prélude', 'Forlane', 'Menuet' and 'Rigaudon' from *Le tombeau de Couperin* (1919).

(c) Recordings

(i) Piano rolls made by Ravel in 1913 for Welte-Mignon (*Sonatine*, movements I and II, C2887; *Valses nobles et sentimentales*, C2888), and in 1922 for Duo-Art (*Pavane pour une Infante défunte*, 084; 'Oiseaux tristes' from *Miroirs*, 082). It was claimed that at this second session Ravel also recorded 'Le gibet' from *Gaspard de la nuit* and the 'Toccata' from *Le tombeau de Couperin*, but these were in fact recorded by Robert Casadesus. It remains uncertain which of the two recorded 'La vallée des cloches' from *Miroirs* in 1929 for Duo-Art (72750), though I am almost certain it was Ravel. All these recordings have been transferred a number of times to LP, but unfortunately the piano roll equipment has not always been properly regulated.

(ii) Recordings made on disc by three pianists, all of whom had the benefit of the composer's detailed advice: Robert Casadesus (1955, CBS 13062–4[3]); Jacques Février (1972, ADES 7041–4); Vlado Perlemuter (1961, VOX VBX 410 1–3[4]; 1977, NIMBUS 2101–3, reissued CD NI 5005, 5011). Marcelle Meyer, although known to Ravel (together they gave the private two-piano performance of *La valse* which failed to impress Diaghilev), never studied his piano music with him, as her daughter, Marie Bertin, was good enough to inform me. I have therefore taken no account of Mme Meyer's Ravel recordings reissued by EMI on the Référence label.

(d) Souvenirs of Ravel as a coach of his piano music

(i) from Vlado Perlemuter in his interviews with Hélène Jourdan-Morhange, published as *Ravel d'après Ravel* (Lausanne, 1953) and in an English translation by F. Tanner as *Ravel according to Ravel* (New York/London, 1988; 2/1991).[5]

(ii) from Vlado Perlemuter in conversation with the editor of the present edition.

(iii) from Henriette Faure in *Mon maître Maurice Ravel* (Paris, 1978) (**FauS**). Mlle Faure, the sister of the politician Edgar Faure, was coached by Ravel for her recital of his music – in all probability the first ever all-Ravel piano recital – which she gave at the Théâtre des Champs-Elysées on 12 January 1923 (not 18 January, as she states in her book), when she was eighteen. Her daughter, Mme Mayette Constantin, kindly informed me that at one time she had in her possession her mother's original notes, taken directly from Ravel's instruction, but that these were lent to a researcher and never returned. Other souvenirs are fully identified *in situ*.

The secondary sources are considered when they shed further light on an established text, or when problems in the text are not fully elucidated by the primary sources.

Acknowledgements

I should like to express my gratitude to the following for their assistance: to Gaby Casadesus for information about her husband Robert; to Dr Michel Noiray, who told me about the autograph of *Sonatine* and helped me to obtain a copy; to James Segesta, reference librarian of California State College, Bakersfield, for sending me copies of Lucien Garban's corrected scores; to Jean Touzelet, and later to Denis Hall and Rex Lawson, for allowing me to hear Ravel's Duo-Art piano rolls on machines in perfect order; and to Dr J. Rigbie Turner, Curator of Music Manuscripts and Books in the Pierpont Morgan Library, New York, for sending me copies of the autographs of *Jeux d'eau*, and of 'Noctuelles' and 'Oiseaux tristes' from *Miroirs*. I am grateful also to various performers; to Vlado Perlemuter for talking to me about his lessons with Ravel and for allowing me to study his copies of the music; to Roy Howat for advice that has blended the scholarly with the practical; to Junko Okazaki for providing me with a photocopy of Perlemuter's copy of the *Valses nobles*; and to Michael Channon, Anthony Goldstone and Charles Timbrell for their views about the tam-tam in 'Laideronnette' and other details in *Ma mère l'oye*. Finally, my thanks go to the staff of the Music Department of the Bibliothèque nationale, and to Margaret Cobb, Graham Hayter, Olivier Mazal, Gwendolyn Mok, Jean-Michel Nectoux, Dr Arbie Orenstein, and Dr Stephen Roe for numerous kindnesses.

[1] Originally Vma. 2967, now reshelved as Rés. Vma. 493
[2] Vma. 3157(7) and Fol. Vm12. 2701(2)A respectively
[3] Reissued SONY MH2K 63316
[4] Reissued VOX CDX2 5507
[5] Dual page numbers refer to the French and English editions respectively

Table of source abbreviations

A: autograph

E: first edition

CE: Ravel's corrected copy of the first edition

PerCE: Perlemuter's printed copy with Ravel's additions and corrections

GarCE: printed copies with Garban's additions and corrections

GarT: Garban's piano duet transcriptions

RO: Ravel's orchestral transcriptions

RR: Ravel's recordings on piano roll

CasR: recordings by Casadesus

FévR: recordings by Février

PerRI and **PerRII**: recordings by Perlemuter[1]

PerS(HJM): souvenirs from Perlemuter in *Ravel d'après Ravel*, in conversation with Hélène Joudan-Morhange[2]

PerS(conv): souvenirs from Perlemuter in conversation with the present Editor

FauS: souvenirs from Fauré in *Mon maître Maurice Ravel*

[1] The designation **PerR** without a number indicates that Perlemuter's two recordings coincide over the point in question
[2] Dual page numbers refer to the French and English editions respectively

GASPARD DE LA NUIT

Preface

It is surprising, perhaps, with all the extra-musical associations to be found in Ravel's piano music – visual ones in *Miroirs*, historical ones in *Valses nobles et sentimentales* and *Le tombeau de Couperin*, not to mention the problem-solving in *Menuet sur le nom d'Haydn* – that only four of his piano works seem to have had direct links with literature. Three of these ('Habanera' from *Sites auriculaires*, *Jeux d'eau* and *Valses nobles et sentimentales*) bear no more than a brief epigraph. *Gaspard de la nuit* is therefore unique among them, not only in taking its title from a collection of prose poems by Aloysius Bertrand, but in being shaped, albeit loosely, by the three poems chosen from the collection by Ravel, which are printed in full at the beginning of each piece in the first edition.

Bertrand (1807–1841) finished *Gaspard de la nuit*, subtitled 'fantaisies à la maniere de Rembrandt et de Callot'[1], in 1836. It was published a year after his death. In his preface Bertrand states that "Art always has two antithetical faces . . . Rembrandt is the white-bearded philosopher who hides away, snail-like, in his retreat, whose thoughts are taken up with meditation and prayer . . . Callot, on the other hand, is the loud-mouthed, loose-living jackanape who swaggers about the square, kicks up a din in the tavern and fondles the gypsies' daughters . . . The author of this book envisaged art under this double personification". In the final paragraph he writes "And if someone asks the author why he does not parade some fine literary theory at the head of his book, he will be forced to reply that . . . Pulcinello keeps his strings hidden from the curious mob. He contents himself with signing his work: GASPARD DE LA NUIT." The volume consists of the preface, an address to Victor Hugo, 51 poems in six books making up 'Les fantaisies de Gaspard de la Nuit', an address to the literary critic Charles-Augustin Sainte-Beuve, and 13 'pieces detachees, extraites du portefeuille de l'auteur'. 'Ondine' comes from the third book of poems entitled 'La nuit et ses prestiges', both 'Le gibet' and 'Scarbo' from the 'pièces détachées'.

Ravel was introduced to the book by his friend Ricardo Viñes (1876–1943) who was a fellow student at the Paris Conservatoire. A Spaniard by birth, Viñes arrived in Paris in 1887 speaking nothing but his own language. Within a few years he had learnt not only French but large portions of French literature by heart, including the whole of Baudelaire's *Les fleurs du mal*. His friendship with Ravel also had a literary as well as a musical basis, as we know from Viñes' diary[2]. In August 1892 Viñes writes that Ravel made two "very sombre" drawings inspired by tales of Edgar Allan Poe (*The Maelstrom* and *Manuscript found in a bottle*) which they were reading together in Baudelaire's translation; and in October 1894 that they were copying out half-a-dozen banned poems from *Les fleurs du mal*. *Gaspard* is first mentioned in the diary on 12 November 1895, when Viñes writes that "he [Ravel] tells me that the *Gaspard de la Nuit* I bought in London is very rare". On 25 September 1896 Viñes allowed Ravel to take the copy away and did not get it back until 20 December 1897, Ravel claiming that it had been at the bottom of a trunk! There are no further entries referring to *Gaspard* until 25 October 1908, when Viñes began to study the music of 'Ondine'. Two days later he played all three pieces to Manuel de Falla and on 8 November he played them again to Albert Roussel. He gave the first public performance in the Salle Erard at a concert of the Société Nationale on 9 January 1909. Press reaction was on the whole favourable.

In being drawn to Poe and Baudelaire, Ravel was very much a young aesthete of his time. Bertrand's credo that "Pulcinello keeps his strings hidden from the curious mob" was also in absolute accordance with his own predilections. But the picture of Ravel as the embodiment of clarity and precision, as a dandy or, in Stravinsky's words, "a Swiss clockmaker", does not really square with some of his pronouncements over *Gaspard*. Hélène Jourdan-Morhange relays a conversation with Viñes in which the pianist says that in 'Ondine' the theme should not stand out but be absorbed into the surrounding atmosphere, and that provided this atmosphere was maintained, Ravel did not worry about the odd wrong note[3]. The pianist Paul Loyonnet remembers Ravel saying about 'Ondine', "If you don't count the exact number of rhythms in the opening figure, it doesn't matter."[4]

There is reason to think that Ravel imitated Bertrand's principle of contrast by making the central piece as different from the outer ones as possible – a Rembrandt between two Callots. He insisted that 'Le gibet' be played monotonously and at an absolutely unvarying tempo. In a letter to the critic M. D. Calvocoressi of 24 March 1922, when he was preparing to make his piano roll recordings for Duo-Art in London, he wrote "I am particularly keen to have *Gaspard de la nuit* on record and Viñes has never seen fit to play these pieces, 'Le gibet' in particular, in the way the composer intended. And I mean seen fit: I don't know whether you have been present at any of those discussions when he has assured me that if he observed the nuances and speeds I wanted, 'Le gibet' would bore the audience to death. He has remained intransigent over this."[5] To Henriette Faure Ravel said that the bell must not be louder that its surroundings: "This bell does not dominate, it is, it tolls unwearyingly."[6]

In the outer movements, on the other hand, he insisted on the contrasts of dynamics being observed[7]. Whatever Viñes' shortcomings as an interpreter, we have no cause to disbelieve him when he says that Ravel wanted the crescendos to be very pronounced, and that pianists in general begin them too early[8]. The spirit of Franz Liszt too hovers over these pieces, and Ravel recommended to Mlle Faure that she work at Liszt's *Feux follets* to correct the heaviness of her thumbs in 'Ondine'[9]. He also asked her not to play too loud overall in 'Scarbo'[10], probably to allow the climaxes to strike home. Some remarks made to other colleagues go a little further in illuminating his intentions in 'Scarbo'. To Henri Gil-Marchex he suggested that the right-hand phrase in bar 32 could be fitted to the words "Quelle horreur!"[11]; he told Maurice Delage that he had wanted to write a work more difficult than Balakirev's *Islamey*[12]; and to Vlado Perlemuter he said "I wanted to compose a caricature of Romanticism", and then in a whisper, "but perhaps I let myself get carried away!"[13]

Finally, the function of 'Le gibet' as a contrast to the other pieces is supported by Ravel's choice of dedicatees. The two outer ones are both dedicated to pianists, 'Ondine' to Harold Bauer and 'Scarbo' to Rudolph Ganz. But 'Le gibet' is dedicated to the critic Jean Marnold who, when other critics such as Pierre Lalo were dismissing Ravel as a mere imitator of Debussy, had defended Ravel's position as an important and original artist. After the first performance of *Gaspard de la nuit*, such a defence was no longer necessary.

Editorial Practice

Square brackets have been applied to the majority of editorial additions: accidentals, notes and rests, time signatures, tempo and pedal markings, dynamics, and *main droite/main gauche* indications. Precautionary accidentals in round brackets, from the first edition (**E**), have, where considered helpful, been retained. The fingerings are all taken from Ravel's corrected copy of the first edition (**CE**) except where otherwise indicated in the Critical Commentary.

The following editorial amendments have been made without their being distinguished in the music text or detailed in the Critical Commentary:

Phrase marks and slurs have been added or amended so as to conform with parallel passages. Similarly, by analogy with corresponding passages, staccato dots/dashes, accents and tenuto markings, in 'Le gibet' and 'Scarbo', have been added or deleted. In 'Le gibet', ties to the lower B♭s of the repeated octave 'bell' pattern, where absent in the sources, have been consistently applied throughout. Source **E** contains some misplacements of such ties which could cause them to be misinterpreted as slurs; the correct positioning of ties and slurs in the present edition eradicates this ambiguity. All irrational rhythmic groupings are here indicated as such; only a few triplet markings appear in the sources.

Roger Nichols, 1991

---

[1]Jacques Callot (1592-1635) was a celebrated engraver. Among his best-known works are *Les misères de la guerre* and *Les tentations de St Antoine*

[2]'Le journal inédit de Ricardo Viñes', ed. N. Gubisch, *Revue Internationale de Musique Fraçaise*, (June 1980), 155–248 [3]H. Jourdan-Morhange: *Ravel et nous*, (Geneva, 1945), 215–16

[4]C. Timbrell: 'An interview with Paul Loyonnet', *Journal of the American Liszt Society*, xix (1986), 112–21

[5]Music Department, Bibliothèque Nationale, Paris, LA Ravel 99

M. Ravel: *Lettres, écrits, entretiens*, ed. A. Orenstein, (Paris, 1989; Eng. trans. A. Orenstein, New York, 1990), 196–97

[6]FauS 61

[7]*ibid* 65

[8]*see* (3)

[9]FauS 57

[10]*ibid* 65

[11]Henri Gil-Marchex: 'Les Concertos de Ravel', *La Revue Musicale*, (Dec 1938), 89

[12]Roland-Manuel: *A la gloire de Ravel*), (Paris, 1938; Eng. trans. C. Jolly, London, 1947, R/1972), 54

[13]**PerS(HJM)** 36/35

LA MUSIQUE POUR PIANO DE RAVEL – UNE NOUVELLE ÉDITION
Principes d'édition et sources

Nul ne niera combien il est émouvant de tenir en main le manuscrit autographe d'un chef-d'œuvre musical ; et lorsque l'autographe est lui-même une œuvre d'art, comme c'est souvent le cas de ceux de Ravel, cette émotion est encore renforcée par les considérations esthétiques. Mais nul ne niera non plus que les compositeurs sont, comme tous les mortels, faillibles, et qu'un autographe, si beau et si émouvant soit-il, peut néanmoins comporter des erreurs. Le désir louable de retourner à ce que le compositeur a écrit à l'origine demande donc à être tempéré par un certain bon sens.

Avec les œuvres scéniques, il est vrai que les questions de temps, de lieu, d'argent et de personnes conduisent souvent à des déformations dont le compositeur ne se réjouit nullement, mais qu'il doit accepter pour que la représentation aille de l'avant, et qui peuvent se trouver incorporées à la partition imprimée. Mais, dans le cas d'œuvres pour piano, les pressions sur le compositeur dans la préparation d'une édition sont bien moindres, exercées pour l'essentiel par l'éditeur, qui souhaite qu'elle se conforme aux usages de la maison, si bien que les changements introduits entre le manuscrit et l'édition ont une plus grande chance de représenter des décisions librement prises par le compositeur. Certes, dans le processus de publication, des erreurs peuvent aussi bien être introduites que rectifiées, et lorsque la musicalité et le bon sens indiquent que c'est le cas, l'autographe peut effectivement apporter un témoignage crucial. Mais des conversations avec un certain nombre de compositeurs de notre temps m'ont convaincu qu'ils seraient en fait très agacés si les futurs éditeurs ignoraient leurs partitions soigneusement préparées et retourneraient automatiquement à leurs autographes originaux pour une lecture prétendument véridique.

Dans le cas de la musique pour piano de Ravel, une telle vision critique des documents autographes est plus que jamais justifiée, puisque le département de la musique de la Bibliothèque nationale de France possède un volume contenant les exemplaires imprimés de Ravel lui-même, avec des corrections autographes, de la plupart des premières éditions de sa musique pour piano seul [1]. À en juger d'après le contenu, le volume semble avoir été réuni entre 1911 et 1913. Les œuvres qui manquent dans cette collection sont : *Sérénade grotesque*, *Sites auriculaires*, *Ma mère l'Oye*, *Prélude*, *À la manière de…*, *Le Tombeau de Couperin* et *Frontispice*. La même bibliothèque conserve séparément des exemplaires imprimés avec corrections autographes de *Ma mère l'Oye* et d'*À la manière de…* [2], tandis que l'exemplaire imprimé personnel de Ravel du *Tombeau de Couperin*, avec doigtés autographes et une correction autographe, est exposé au musée Ravel de Monfort-l'Amaury. Pour la *Sérénade grotesque* et les *Sites auriculaires*, les autographes sont d'une importance capitale, puisque ces œuvres ne furent pas publiées du vivant du compositeur. L'autographe de *Frontispice* est également important, puisque l'on n'a pas retrouvé l'exemplaire imprimé de Ravel. Malheureusement, pour le *Prélude*, ni l'autographe ni l'exemplaire imprimé du compositeur ne nous sont parvenus.

À notre connaissance, il ne subsiste d'épreuves de la première édition d'aucune œuvre pour piano de Ravel, mis à part une série de premières épreuves du *Tombeau de Couperin* dans les archives Durand, marquées par l'éditeur de Durand d'une demande de secondes épreuves (je remercie Roy Howat de m'avoir fourni une copie de ces documents). Ces épreuves ne comportent pas d'indications autographes. Toutes les annotations éditoriales ont été intégrées à la première édition sauf la forme de certaines des appoggiatures multiples dans le « Prélude » et la « Forlane » du *Tombeau de Couperin*, au sujet desquelles Ravel semblerait avoir changé d'avis.

Sources primaires

Lorsque l'édition corrigée de Ravel est disponible, je l'ai prise comme source primaire principale ; les divergences entre cette édition corrigée (**CE**), la première édition imprimée (**E**) et l'autographe sont dûment notées.

L'autographe des *Valses nobles* (neuf pages dans la collection Taverne) n'est pas disponible pour étude, mais un microfilm (**AM**) est conservé au département de la musique de la Bibliothèque nationale de France (Vm. micr. 876).

Sources secondaires

Les sources secondaires se divisent en quatre groupes :

(a) Exemplaires imprimés avec corrections de musiciens proches de Ravel :

(i) Exemplaires de la musique de piano de Ravel ayant appartenu à Robert Casadesus (**CasCE**), maintenant conservés au département de la musique de la BnF ; son exemplaire des *Valses nobles* est coté Vm. Casadesus 940. Il ne comporte pas d'indications de la main du compositeur.

(ii) Quelques exemplaires, dont celui des *Valses nobles*, ayant appartenu à Vlado Perlemuter (**PerCE**), maintenant également conservés à la BnF, mais en attente de catalogage.

(iii) Quelques exemplaires imprimés avec corrections de Lucien Garban. Garban, qui travaillait pour la maison d'édition Durand, était un ami intime du compositeur. Le statut exact de ces corrections est impossible à déterminer, mais, étant donné les liens entre les deux hommes, il est possible qu'au moins certains des changements aient été dictés par Ravel. Ces exemplaires sont maintenant à la bibliothèque de Bakersfield College, Californie. Garban fit également des transcriptions pour piano à quatre mains des *Valses nobles et sentimentales* et du *Tombeau de Couperin*. Elles sont publiées par Durand.

(iv) Parmi les exemplaires qui n'ont pas été consultés figurent ceux de Jacques Février, dont la nièce et élève, Mme Aboulker-Rosenfeld, m'a assuré qu'ils ne comportaient pas d'autres indications que ses doigtés ; et ceux d'Henriette Faure, qui n'ont pu être retrouvés.

(b) Les orchestrations faites par Ravel lui-même d'un certain nombre de ses œuvres pour piano (**RO**). Par ordre chronologique des compositions originales (dates d'orchestration entre parenthèses), ce sont : *Menuet antique* (1929), « Habanera » des *Sites auriculaires* (1908), *Pavane pour une infante défunte* (1910), « Une barque sur l'océan » et « Alborada del gracioso » de *Miroirs* (1906 et 1923), *Ma mère l'Oye* (1911), *Valses nobles et sentimentales* (1912), « Prélude », « Forlane », « Menuet » et « Rigaudon » du *Tombeau de Couperin* (1919).

(c) Enregistrements

(i) Rouleaux de piano faits par Ravel en 1913 pour Welte-Mignon (*Sonatine*, mouvements I et II, C2887 ; *Valses nobles et sentimentales*, C2888) et en 1922 pour Duo-Art (*Pavane pour une infante défunte*, 084 ; « Oiseaux tristes » de *Miroirs*, 082). On a dit que lors de cette seconde séance Ravel enregistra également « Le Gibet » de *Gaspard de la nuit* et la « Toccata » du *Tombeau de Couperin*, mais ces pièces furent en fait enregistrées par Robert Casadesus. On ne sait pas avec certitude lequel des deux enregistra « La Vallée des cloches » de *Miroirs* en 1929 pour Duo-Art (72750), encore que je sois presque sûr que c'est Ravel. Tous ces enregistrements ont été transférés un certain nombre de fois sur microsillon, mais malheureusement à partir de pianos mécaniques qui n'étaient pas toujours bien réglés.

(ii) Enregistrements faits sur disque par trois pianistes qui bénéficièrent tous de conseils détaillés du compositeur : Robert Casadesus (1955, CBS 13062-4 [3]) ; Jacques Février (1972, ADES 7041-4) ; Vlado Perlemuter (1961, VOX VBX 410 1-3 [4] ; 1977, NIMBUS 2101-3, réédition en CD NI 5005, 5011). Marcelle Meyer, qui connaissait Ravel (ils donnèrent ensemble l'exécution à deux pianos de *La Valse* qui ne réussit pas à impressionner Diaghilev), n'étudia jamais sa musique pour piano avec lui, comme sa fille, Marie Bertin, a bien voulu me le confirmer. Je n'ai donc pas tenu compte des enregistrements Ravel de Marcelle Meyer réédités chez EMI dans la collection Référence. Mais je me suis bien entendu référé à l'enregistrement de *Ma mère l'Oye* signé par Casadesus avec son épouse Gaby (1951, Sony Classical MH2K 63316) (**CasrgR**).

(d) Souvenirs de conseils donnés par Ravel sur l'interprétation de sa musique pour piano et rapportés par :

(i) Vlado Perlemuter dans ses entretiens avec Hélène Jourdan-Morhange, publiés sous le titre *Ravel d'après Ravel* (Lausanne, 1953) ;

(ii) Vlado Perlemuter dans des entretiens avec moi-même ;

(iii) Henriette Faure dans *Mon maître Maurice Ravel* (Paris, 1978) (**FauS**). Ravel fit travailler Henriette Faure, sœur de l'homme politique Edgar Faure, pour le récital – très probablement le tout premier récital de piano entièrement consacré à Ravel – qu'elle donna au théâtre des Champs-Élysées le 12 janvier 1923 (et non le 18 janvier, comme elle le dit dans son livre), à l'âge de dix-huit ans. Sa fille, Mme Mayette Constantin, m'a aimablement informé qu'à une époque elle avait en sa possession les notes originales de sa mère, directement tirées de l'enseignement de Ravel, mais qu'elle les prêta à un chercheur qui ne les lui rendit jamais. Les références d'autres souvenirs sont données dans le texte.

Les sources secondaires sont prises en compte lorsqu'elles jettent une lumière nouvelle sur un texte établi, ou lorsque des problèmes de texte ne sont pas pleinement élucidés par les sources primaires.

Remerciements

J'aimerais remercier les personnes suivantes pour leur aide : Gaby Casadesus, pour les renseignements sur son mari Robert ; Michel Noiray, qui m'a parlé de l'autographe de la *Sonatine* et m'a aidé à en obtenir une copie ; James Segesta, bibliothécaire de California State College, Bakersfield, qui m'a envoyé des copies des partitions corrigées de Lucien Garban ; Jean Touzelet, et ensuite Denis Hall et Rex Lawson, qui m'ont permis d'entendre les rouleaux de piano Duo-Art de Ravel sur des machines en parfait état ; et J. Rigbie Turner, conservateur des manuscrits et livres musicaux de la Pierpont Morgan Library, New York, qui m'a fait parvenir des copies des autographes de *Jeux d'eau*, et de « Noctuelles » et « Oiseaux tristes » de *Miroirs*. Ma reconnaissance va également à divers interprètes : à Vlado Perlemuter, qui m'a parlé de ses leçons avec Ravel et m'a permis d'étudier ses partitions ; à Roy Howat, qui m'a donné des conseils à la fois musicologiques et pratiques ; à Junko Okazaki, qui m'a fourni une photocopie de l'exemplaire des *Valses nobles* de Perlemuter ; et à Michael Channon, Anthony Goldstone et Charles Timbrell, pour leurs idées sur le tam-tam dans « Laideronnette » et d'autres détails dans *Ma mère l'Oye*. Enfin, ma gratitude va au personnel du département de la musique de la Bibliothèque nationale de France, ainsi qu'à Margaret Cobb, Graham Hayter, Olivier Mazal, Gwendolyn Mok, Jean-Michel Nectoux, Arbie Orenstein et Stephen Roe pour leurs nombreuses gentillesses.

[1] À l'origine Vma. 2967, maintenant recoté Rés. Vma. 493.

[2] Vma. 3157(7) et Fol. Vm12. 2701(2)A respectivement.

[3] Réédition SONY MH2K 63316.

[4] Réédition VOX CDX2 5507.

Table des abréviations des sources

A : autographe
E : première édition
CE : exemplaire corrigé de la première édition ayant appartenu à Ravel
PerCE : exemplaire imprimé de Perlemuter avec les additions et corrections de Ravel
GarCE : exemplaires imprimés avec les additions et corrections de Garban
GarT : transcriptions pour piano à quatre mains de Garban
RO : transcriptions orchestrales de Ravel
RR : enregistrements de Ravel sur rouleau de piano
CasR : enregistrements de Casadesus
FévR : enregistrements de Février
PerRI et **PerRII** : enregistrements de Perlemuter [1]
PerS(HJM) : souvenirs de Perlemuter dans *Ravel d'après Ravel*, entretiens avec Hélène Jourdan-Morhange [2]
PerS(conv) : souvenirs de Perlemuter, entretiens avec moi-même
FauS : souvenirs d'Henriette Faure, dans *Mon maître Maurice Ravel*

[1] La mention **PerR** sans chiffre indique que les deux enregistrements de Perlemuter coïncident sur le point en question.

[2] Les numéros de page doubles renvoient aux éditions française et anglaise, respectivement.

GASPARD DE LA NUIT

Préface

Il est sans doute surprenant, au vu de toutes les associations extramusicales qu'on trouve dans la musique pour piano de Ravel – visuelles dans *Miroirs*, historiques dans les *Valses nobles et sentimentales* et *Le Tombeau de Couperin*, pour ne rien dire de l'énigme à résoudre dans le *Menuet sur le nom d'Haydn* –, que seules quatre de ses œuvres pour piano semblent avoir des liens directs avec la littérature. Trois d'entre elles (la « Habanera » des *Sites auriculaires*, *Jeux d'eau* et les *Valses nobles et sentimentales*) ne comportent qu'une brève épigraphe. *Gaspard de la nuit* est donc unique parmi elles, non seulement en empruntant son titre à un recueil de poèmes en prose d'Aloysius Bertrand, mais en étant façonné, quoique librement, par les trois poèmes choisis par Ravel dans le recueil, imprimés en entier au début de chaque pièce dans la première édition.

Bertrand (1807-1841) acheva *Gaspard de la nuit,* sous-titré « fantaisies à la maniere de Rembrandt et de Callot [1] », en 1836. Le recueil fut publié un an après sa mort. Dans sa préface, Bertrand affirme : « L'art a toujours deux faces antithétiques [...]. Rembrandt est le philosophe à barbe blanche qui s'encolimaçonne en son réduit, qui absorbe sa pensée dans la méditation et dans la prière [...]. Callot, au contraire, est le lansquenet fanfaron et grivois qui se pavane sur la place, qui fait du bruit dans la taverne, qui caresse les filles de bohémiens [...]. L'auteur de ce livre a envisagé l'art sous cette double personification. » Et dans le dernier paragraphe il ajoute : « Et que si on demande à l'auteur pourquoi il ne parangonne point en tête de son ouvrage quelque belle théorie littéraire, il sera forcé de répondre que M. Séraphin ne lui a pas expliqué le mécanisme de ses ombres chinoises, et que Polichinelle cache à la foule curieuse le fil conducteur de son bras. – Il se contente de signer son œuvre : GASPARD DE LA NUIT. » Le volume consiste en cette préface, une dédicace à Victor Hugo, cinquante et un poèmes en six livres composant « Les fantaisies de Gaspard de la nuit », une dédicace au critique littéraire Charles-Augustin Sainte-Beuve, et treize « pièces détachées, extraites du portefeuille de l'auteur ». « Ondine » provient du troisième livre de poèmes, intitulé « La Nuit et ses prestiges » ; « Le Gibet » et « Scarbo », tous deux des « pièces détachées ».

C'est son ami Ricardo Viñes (1876-1943), condisciple au Conservatoire de Paris, qui fit découvrir le livre à Ravel. Espagnol de naissance, Viñes était arrivé à Paris en 1887 en ne parlant que sa propre langue. En l'espace de quelques années, il avait non seulement appris le français, mais savait par cœur de grands fragments de littérature française, dont l'intégralité des *Fleurs du mal* de Baudelaire. Son amitié avec Ravel reposait sur une base aussi bien littéraire que musicale, comme nous l'apprend le journal de Viñes [2]. En août 1892, Viñes écrit que Ravel fit deux dessins « très sombres » inspirés par des contes d'Edgar Allan Poe (*Une descente dans le Maelstrom* et *Manuscrit trouvé dans une bouteille*) qu'ils lisaient ensemble dans la traduction de Baudelaire ; et, en octobre 1894, qu'ils copiaient une demi-douzaine de poèmes censurés des *Fleurs du mal*. *Gaspard* est cité pour la première fois dans le journal le 12 novembre 1895, où Viñes écrit : « [Ravel] m'a dit que le *Gaspard de la Nuit* que j'ai acheté à Londres est très rare. » Le 25 septembre 1896, Viñes autorisa Ravel à emporter cet exemplaire, qu'il ne recouvra que le 20 décembre 1897, car Ravel affirmait qu'il était au fond d'une malle ! Il n'y a pas d'autres références à *Gaspard* avant le 25 octobre 1908, quand Viñes commence à étudier la musique d'« Ondine ». Deux jours plus tard, il joue les trois pièces à Manuel de Falla, et, le 8 novembre, il les joue de nouveau pour Albert Roussel. Il en donne la première exécution publique à la Salle Érard, lors d'un concert de la Société nationale, le 9 janvier 1909. La réaction de la presse est dans l'ensemble favorable.

Séduit par Poe et Baudelaire, Ravel était tout à fait un jeune esthète de son temps. Le credo de Bertrand – « Polichinelle cache à la foule curieuse le fil conducteur de son bras » – était absolument en accord avec ses propres convictions. Mais l'image de Ravel en incarnation de la clarté et de la précision, en dandy ou, selon le mot de Stravinsky, en « horloger suisse », ne concorde pas vraiment avec certaines de ses déclarations sur *Gaspard*. Hélène Jourdan-Morhange rapporte ainsi une conversation avec Viñes dans laquelle le pianiste lui dit que, dans « Ondine », le thème ne devait pas ressortir, mais être asborbé dans l'atmosphère environnante, et que, pourvu que cette atmosphère soit préservée, Ravel ne s'inquiétait pas d'une occasionnelle fausse note [3]. Le pianiste Paul Loyonnet raconte que Ravel disait au sujet d'« Ondine », que si, dans le trait du début, on ne comptait pas précisément le nombre de rythmes, cela importait peu [4].

Il y a de bonnes raisons de penser que Ravel imita le principe de contraste de Bertrand en concevant une pièce centrale aussi différente que possible des deux qui l'encadrent – un Rembrandt entre deux Callot. Il tenait à ce que « Le Gibet » soit joué de manière monotone, et à un tempo absolument constant. Dans une lettre au critique M. D. Calvocoressi du 24 mars 1922, alors qu'il s'apprêtait à faire ses enregistrements sur rouleau de piano pour Duo-Art à Londres, il écrivit : « Je voudrais surtout faire enregistrer *Gaspard de la nuit* et [...] Viñes n'a jamais voulu exécuter ces pièces et singulièrement "Le Gibet" de telle manière que l'auteur le désirait. Je dis bien *voulu* : je ne sais si vous avez assisté à l'une de ces discussions où il m'assurait que, s'il observait les nuances et les mouvements que je voulais, "Le Gibet" embêterait le public. Il n'a jamais voulu en démordre [5]. » À Henriette Faure, Ravel confia que la cloche ne doit pas être plus forte que son environnement : « Cette cloche ne domine pas, elle est, elle tinte inlassablement [6]. »

Dans les mouvements extrêmes, en revanche, il tenait à ce que les contrastes de nuances soient respectés [7]. Quelles que soient les insuffisances de Viñes en tant qu'interprète, nous n'avons aucune raison de ne pas le croire quand il dit que Ravel voulait que les crescendos soient très prononcés, et que les pianistes les commencent en général trop tôt [8]. L'esprit de Franz Liszt plane aussi sur ces pièces, et Ravel conseilla du reste à Mlle Faure de travailler *Feux follets* de Liszt pour corriger la lourdeur de ses pouces dans « Ondine » [9]. Il lui demanda également de ne pas jouer trop fort en général dans « Scarbo » [10], probablement pour laisser les gradations produire leur plein effet. Certaines remarques faites à d'autres collègues vont un peu plus loin, en éclairant ses intentions dans « Scarbo ». À Gil-Marchex, il expliqua ainsi que la phrase de main droite à la mesure 32 pouvait être pensée sur les mots « Quelle horreur ! » [11] ; il dit à Maurice Delage qu'il avait voulu écrire une œuvre plus difficile qu'*Islamey* de Balakirev [12] ; et à Vlado Perlemuter, il confia : « J'ai voulu faire une caricature du romantisme » ; avant d'ajouter tout bas : « Je m'y suis peut-être laissé prendre [13]. »

Enfin, la fonction de contraste de la pièce centrale, « Le Gibet », avec les deux autres est confirmée par le choix des dédicataires. Ravel dédia les deux pièces extrêmes à des pianistes – « Ondine » à Harold Bauer et « Scarbo » à Rudolph Ganz. Mais « Le Gibet » est dédié au critique Jean Marnold, qui, alors que d'autres critiques tel Pierre Lalo condamnaient Ravel comme un simple imitateur de Debussy, avait défendu la position de Ravel en tant qu'artiste important et original. Après la création de *Gaspard de la nuit,* une telle défense n'était plus nécessaire.

Principes éditoriaux

La plupart des ajouts de l'éditeur sont entre crochets : altérations, notes et silences, indications de mesure, de tempo et de pédale, nuances, et indications *main droite et main gauche*. Les altérations de précaution entre parenthèses de la première édition (**E**) ont été conservées lorsqu'elles ont été jugées utiles. Les doigtés proviennent tous de l'exemplaire corrigé de la première édition de Ravel lui-même (**CE**), sauf indication contraire dans le commentaire critique.

Les corrections éditoriales suivantes ont été faites sans qu'elles soient indiquées dans le texte musical ou dans le commentaire critique :

Des indications de phrasé et des liaisons ont été ajoutées ou corrigérs pour la concordance des passages parallèles. De même, par analogie avec les passages correspondants, des points ou traits de staccato, des accents et des signes de tenuto, dans « Le Gibet » et « Scarbo », ont été ajoutés ou supprimés. Dans « Le Gibet », les liaisons entre les *si* graves du motif répété de cloche en octaves ont été ajoutées systématiquement quand elles manquent dans les sources. La source **E** contient certaines fautes de placement de telles tenues qui pourraient amener à les interpréter à tort comme des liaisons de phrasé ; la place correcte des liaisons de prolongation et de phrasé dans la présente édition élimine cette ambiguïté. Tous les groupements rythmiques irrationnels sont ici indiqués en tant que tels ; seules quelques triolets sont marqués dans les sources.

Roger Nichols, 1991
Traduction : Dennis Collins

---

1. Jacques Callot (1592-1635) était un célèbre graveur. *Les Misères de la guerre* et *Les Tentations de saint Antoine* sont parmi ses œuvres les plus connues.

2. « Le journal inédit de Ricardo Vines », éd. N. Gubisch, *Revue internationale de musique française* (juin 1980), p. 155-248.

3. H. Jourdan-Morhange, *Ravel et nous* (Genève, 1945), p. 215-216.

4. C. Timbrell, « An interview with Paul Loyonnet », *Journal of the American Liszt Society*, xix (1986), p. 112-121

5. Département de la musique, Bibliotheque nationale de France, Paris, LA Ravel 99. M. Ravel, *Lettres, écrits, entretiens*, éd. A. Orenstein (Paris, 1989), p. 197.

6. **FauS,** p. 61.

7. *Ibid.* p. 65.

8. Voir (3).

9. **FauS,** p. 57.

10. *Ibid.* p. 65.

11. Henri Gil-Marchex, « Les Concertos de Ravel », *La Revue musicale* (décembre 1938), p. 89.

12. Roland-Manuel, *À la gloire de Ravel*, Paris, 1938

13. **PerS(HJM),** p. 36/p. 35.

RAVELS KLAVIERMUSIK – NEUE AUSGABE
Editorische Methode und Quellen

Es ist nicht zu leugnen, dass sich ein Gefühl der Aufregung einstellt, wenn man die autographe Handschrift eines musikalischen Meisterwerks in Händen hält, und wenn darüber hinaus das Autograph selbst ein Kunstwerk ist, wie bei Ravel oft der Fall, so wird dieses Gefühl durch ästhetische Eindrücke noch verstärkt. Ebenso wenig ist jedoch zu leugnen, dass Komponisten wie alle Sterblichen fehlbar sind, und dass das Autograph, so schön und aufregend es sein mag, Fehler enthalten kann. Das scheinbar löbliche Unterfangen, auf das zurückzugreifen, was der Komponist ursprünglich schrieb, muss daher mit einer gewissen Portion Allgemeinverstand aufgewogen werden.

Bei Bühnenwerken führen zeitliche, räumliche, finanzielle und persönliche Zwänge ohne Frage oft zu Eingriffen, die der Komponist in keiner Weise begrüßt, die er aber billigen muss, will er die Aufführung nicht gefährden, und die so in die gedruckte Partitur gelangen. Im Falle von Klavierwerken ist der Druck auf den Komponisten bei der Vorbereitung einer Ausgabe jedoch wesentlich geringer (und wird vor allem vom Verleger ausgeübt, der den Verlagsrichtlinien zu entsprechen sucht), so dass Änderungen auf dem Wege von der Handschrift zur Druckausgabe mit größerer Wahrscheinlichkeit dem Willen des Komponisten entsprechen. Natürlich können im Verlauf der Drucklegung Fehler sowohl entstehen als auch korrigiert werden, und wenn allgemeine und musikalische Erwägungen dies vermuten lassen, kann sich das Autograph tatsächlich oft als ein wichtiges Indiz erweisen. In Gesprächen mit zahlreichen Komponisten der Gegenwart aber wurde mir ganz überwiegend versichert, dass sie vielmehr verärgert wären, würden zukünftige Herausgeber ihre sorgsam erarbeiteten gedruckten Partituren übergehen und auf der Suche nach einer angeblich korrekten Lesart automatisch auf ihre originalen Manuskripte zurückgreifen.

Im Falle von Ravels Klaviermusik ist ein solch kritischer Umgang mit handschriftlichen Zeugnissen mehr denn je gerechtfertigt, findet sich doch in der Musikabteilung der Bibliothèque Nationale de France eine gebundene Sammlung von Ravels eigenen Exemplaren fast aller gedruckten Erstausgaben seiner Solowerke für Klavier samt autographer Korrekturen[1]. Dem Inhalt nach zu urteilen wurde der Band wohl zwischen

1911 und 1913 zusammengestellt. Bei den fehlenden Werken handelt es sich um die *Sérénade grotesque*, *Sites auriculaires*, *Ma mère l'oye*, *Prélude*, *A la manière de…*, *Le tombeau de Couperin* und *Frontispice*. Gedruckte Ausgaben von *Ma mère l'oye* und *A la manière de…* mit autographen Korrekturen finden sich an anderem Ort in derselben Bibliothek[2], während Ravels eigenes Druckexemplar von *Le tombeau de Couperin* mit eigenhändigen Fingersätzen und einer einzigen autographen Korrektur im Musée Ravel in Montfort l'Amaury ausgestellt ist. Bei der *Sérénade grotesque* und *Sites auriculaires* können die Autographen als vorrangige Quellen betrachtet werden, da diese Werke nicht zu Lebzeiten des Komponisten veröffentlicht wurden. Die Eigenschrift von *Frontispice* ist ebenfalls von Bedeutung, da Ravels eigene gedruckte Ausgabe verschollen ist. Für *Prélude* liegt leider weder das Autograph noch das Druckexemplar des Komponisten vor.

Nach aktuellem Kenntnisstand existieren keine Korrekturabzüge der Erstausgaben von Ravels Klavierwerken außer einem Satz Erstkorrekturfahnen von *Le tombeau de Couperin* im Archiv von Durand, die von einem Durand-Lektor berichtet und mit einer Bitte um Zweitkorrekturabzüge versehen wurden. (Herzlich möchte ich Roy Howat danken, der mir eine Kopie dieses Materials zur Verfügung stellte.) Dieser Satz enthält keine autographen Eintragungen. Sämtliche Korrekturanweisungen wurden in der Erstausgabe berücksichtigt, mit Ausnahme der Gestaltung einiger Mehrfach-Vorschläge in „Prélude" und „Forlane" von *Le tombeau de Couperin*, bezüglich derer augenscheinlich Ravel seine Meinung änderte.

Hauptquellen

Wo Ravels eigenes korrigiertes Exemplar verfügbar war, wurde dieses als Hauptquelle zugrunde gelegt; Abweichungen zwischen dieser korrigierten Ausgabe (**CE**), der gedruckten Erstausgabe (**E**) und dem Autograph sind entsprechend vermerkt. Das neunseitige Autograph der *Valses nobles* (in der Sammlung Taverne) ist zu Forschungszwecken bislang nicht zugänglich, doch existiert ein Mikrofilm (**AM**) in der Musikabteilung der Bibliothèque nationale de France (Vm. micr. 876).

Nebenquellen

Die Nebenquellen gliedern sich in vier Gruppen:

(a) Druckexemplare mit Korrekturen von Musikern aus Ravels Umfeld

(I) Ausgaben von Ravels Klavierwerken aus dem Besitz von Robert Casadesus (**CasCE**), nunmehr ebenfalls in der Musikabteilung der BNF verwahrt; sein Exemplar der *Valses nobles* findet sich unter der Signatur Vm. Casadesus 940. Es enthält keine Eintragungen von Hand des Komponisten.

(II) Einige Exemplare, unter anderem jenes der *Valses nobles*, aus dem Besitz von Vlado Perlemuter (**PerCE**), nun ebenfalls im Bestand der BNF, jedoch bisher nicht katalogisiert.

(III) Einige Exemplare mit Korrekturen von Lucien Garban. Garban arbeitete für den Verlag Durand und war ein enger Freund des Komponisten. Der genaue Rang dieser Korrekturen ist nicht festzustellen, doch angesichts der Verbindung der beiden ist es denkbar, dass zumindest ein Teil der Änderungen auf Ravel zurückgeht. Diese Exemplare befinden sich nun in der der Bibliothek des Bakersfield College in Kalifornien. Garban bearbeitete darüber hinaus die *Valses nobles et sentimentales* sowie *Le tombeau de Couperin* für Klavier zu vier Händen. Diese Transkriptionen werden bei Durand verlegt.

(IV) Zu den Ausgaben, die nicht herangezogen wurden, gehören jene aus dem Besitz von Jacques Février, dessen Nichte und Schülerin Mme Aboulker-Rosenfeld mir versicherte, dass sie über seine Fingersätze hinaus keine Eintragungen enthielten, sowie jene von Henriette Faure, die verschollen sind.

(b) Ravels eigene Orchestrierungen etlicher seiner Klavierstücke (**RO**). In chronologischer Reihenfolge der Erstkomposition (Jahr der Orchestrierung in Klammern) umfassen diese: das *Menuet antique* (1929), die „Habanera" aus *Sites auriculaires* (1908), *Pavane pour une Infante défunte* (1910), „Une barque sur l'océan" und „Alborada del gracioso" aus den *Miroirs* (1906 und 1923), *Ma mère l'oye* (1911), *Valses nobles et sentimentales* (1912) sowie „Prélude", „Forlane", „Menuet" und „Rigaudon" aus *Le tombeau de Couperin* (1919).

(c) Einspielungen

(I) Klavierrollen, die Ravel 1913 für Welte-Mignon einspielte (*Sonatine*, 1. und 2. Satz, C2887; *Valses nobles et sentimentales*, C2888) und 1922 für Duo-Art (*Pavane pur une Infante défunte*, 084; „Oiseaux tristes" aus den *Miroirs*, 082). Es ist behauptet worden, dass Ravel bei dieser zweiten Gelegenheit auch „Le gibet" aus *Gaspard de la nuit* und die „Toccata" aus *Le tombeau de Couperin* aufgenommen habe, doch wurden diese vielmehr von Robert Casadesus aufgezeichnet. Es bleibt fraglich, welcher der beiden 1929 für Duo-Art „La vallée des cloches" aus *Miroirs* einspielte (72750), obwohl der Herausgeber sich nahezu sicher ist, dass es Ravel war. All diese Einspielungen sind verschiedentlich auf LP übertragen worden, doch leider war die Klavierrollen-Wiedergabe dabei nicht immer optimal eingestellt.

(II) Schallplattenaufnahmen dreier Pianisten, die sämtlich in den Genuss genauer Anweisungen vom Komponisten kamen: Robert Casadesus (1955, CBS 13062-4[3]); Jacques Février (1972, ADES 7041-4); Vlado Perlemuter (1961, VOX VBX 410 1-3[4]; 1977, NIMBUS 2101-3, später erschienen als CD NI 5005, 5011). Marcelle Meyer war zwar mit Ravel bekannt (sie gaben zusammen jene Privataufführung von *La valse* auf zwei Klavieren, welche Diaghilev bekanntermaßen unbeeindruckt ließ), doch studierte sie seine Klavierwerke nie mit ihm ein, wie mir ihre Tochter Marie Bertin freundlicherweise mitteilte. Ich habe daher Mme Meyers Ravel-Aufnahmen, die von EMI beim Label Référence neu veröffentlicht wurden, außer Acht gelassen.

(d) Erinnerungen an Ravel als Vermittler seiner Klaviermusik

(I) von Vlado Perlemuter in seinen Interviews mit Hélène Jourdan-Morhange, veröffentlicht als *Ravel d'après Ravel* (Lausanne 1953) sowie in englischer Übersetzung als *Ravel according to Ravel* (New York/London 1988; 2/1991)[5].

(II) von Vlado Perlemuter im Gespräch mit dem Herausgeber der vorliegenden Ausgabe.

(III) von Henriette Faure in *Mon maître Maurice Ravel* (Paris 1978) (**FauS**). Mlle Faure, die Schwester des Politikers Edgar Faure, nahm anlässlich ihres Recitals seiner Musik im Theâtre des Champs-Elysées am 12. Januar 1923 (nicht am 18. Januar, wie in ihrem Buch behauptet) – wahrscheinlich das erste Recital überhaupt, das ausschließlich Ravel gewidmet war – im Alter von 18 Jahren Unterricht beim Komponisten. Ihre Tochter, Mme Mayette Constantin, teilte mir freundlicherweise mit, dass sie einst im Besitz der originalen Aufzeichnungen ihrer Mutter gewesen sei, die unmittelbar auf Ravels Anweisungen beruhten, dass sie diese jedoch einem Forscher zur Verfügung gestellt und nie zurückerhalten habe. Auf andere Erinnerungen wird an Ort und Stelle verwiesen.

Die Nebenquellen sind immer dort einbezogen, wo sie zusätzliche Erkenntnisse über die etablierte Lesart vermitteln oder wo Probleme des Notentextes nicht anhand der Hauptquellen gelöst werden konnten.

Danksagungen

Ich danke den folgenden Personen für ihre freundliche Unterstützung: Gaby Casadesus für Informationen über ihren Gatten Robert; Dr. Michel Noiray, der mich auf das Autograph der *Sonatine* aufmerksam machte und mir bei der Beschaffung einer Kopie behilflich war; James Segesta, Bibliothekar beim Leserdienst des California State College in Bakersfield, der mir Kopien der korrigierten Exemplare von Lucien Garban zusandte; Jean Touzelet, und später Denis Hall und Rex Lawson, die es mir ermöglichten, Ravels Duo-Art-Klavierrollen auf einwandfrei funktionierenden Geräten anzuhören; und Dr. J. Rigbie Turner, Leiter der Abteilung für Musikhandschriften und -bücher in der Piepont Morgan Library in New York, für die Zusendung von Kopien der Autographen von *Jeux d'Eau* sowie von „Noctuelles" und „Oiseaux tristes" aus *Miroirs*. Darüber hinaus bin ich verschiedenen ausübenden Musikern zu Dank verpflichtet: Vlado Perlemuter, der mit mir über seinen Unterricht bei Ravel sprach und es mir gestattete, seine Notenausgaben durchzusehen; Roy Howat für seine Ratschläge, die stets Wissenschaft und Praxis zu vereinbaren wussten; Junko Okazaki, der mir eine Fotokopie von Perlemuters Exemplar der *Valses nobles* zur Verfügung stellte; sowie

Michael Channon, Anthony Goldstone und Charles Timbrell für ihre Ansichten zum Tamtam in „Laideronette" und anderen Einzelheiten in *Ma mère l'oye*. Schließlich danke ich den Mitarbeitern der Musikabteilung der Bibliothèque Nationale sowie Margaret Cobb, Graham Hayter, Olivier Mazal, Gwendolyn Mok, Jean-Michel Nectoux, Dr. Arbie Orenstein und Dr. Stephen Roe für zahlreiche freundliche Hilfeleistungen.

[1] Ursprünglich Vma. 2967, nunmehr unter der Signatur Rés. Vma. 493.
[2] Vma. 3157(7) bzw. Fol. Vm12. 2701(2)A.
[3] Später erschienen als SONY MH2K 63316.
[4] Später erschienen als VOX CDX2 5507.
[5] Doppelte Seitenangaben beziehen sich jeweils auf die französische und englische Ausgabe.

Verzeichnis der Quellensiglen

A: Autograph

E: Erstausgabe

CE: Ravels korrigiertes Exemplar der Erstausgabe

PerCE: Perlemuters Druckexemplar mit Zusätzen und Korrekturen von Ravel

GarCE: Druckexemplar mit Zusätzen und Korrekturen von Garban

GarT: Garbans Bearbeitungen für Klavier zu vier Händen

RO: Ravels Orchesterbearbeitungen

RR: Ravels Einspielungen auf Klavierrolle

CasR: Einspielungen von Casadesus

FévR: Einspielungen von Février

PerRI und **PerRII**: Einspielungen von Perlemuter[1]

PerS(HJM): Erinnerungen von Perlemuter in Ravel d'après Ravel, im Gespräch mit Hélène Jourdan-Morhange[2]

PerS(conv): Erinnerungen von Perlemuter im Gespräch mit dem Herausgeber

FauS: Erinnerungen von Faure in Mon maître Maurice Ravel

[1] Die Bezeichnung **PerR** ohne Nummer bedeutet, dass die zwei Aufnahmen von Perlemuter in Bezug auf den fraglichen Punkt übereinstimmen.
[2] Doppelte Seitenangaben beziehen sich jeweils auf die französische und englische Ausgabe.

GASPARD DE LA NUIT
Vorwort

Ravels Klaviermusik birgt zahlreiche außermusikalische Inhalte: visuelle in *Miroirs*, historische in *Valses nobles et sentimentales* und *Le tombeau de Couperin*, ganz abgesehen von der kompositionstechnischen Bewältigung selbstgestellter Aufgaben im *Menuet sur le nom d'Haydn*. So mag es erstaunen, dass nur vier seiner Klavierwerke eine direkte Verbindung zur Literatur erkennen lassen. Drei von ihnen (die „Habanera" aus den *Sites auriculaires* sowie *Jeux d'eau* und die *Valses nobles et sentimentales*) tragen nicht mehr als ein poetisches Motto. *Gaspard de la nuit* nimmt daher eine Sonderstellung ein: nicht nur weil sein Titel auf die gleichnamige Sammlung von Prosagedichten von Aloysius Bertrand verweist, sondern auch weil das Stück in seiner – wenngleich freien – Form durch drei von Ravel ausgesuchte Gedichte dieser Sammlung bestimmt ist. In der ersten Ausgabe sind sie jeweils zu Beginn des Satzes in voller Länge abgedruckt.

Untertitelt mit „fantaisies à la maniere de Rembrandt et de Callot"[1], vollendete Bertrand (1807–1841) Gaspard de la nuit im Jahr 1836. Die Sammlung wurde ein Jahr nach seinem Tode veröffentlicht. Im Vorwort hält Bertrand fest: „Die Kunst hat immer zwei entgegengesetzte Gesichter. […] Rembrandt ist der weißbärtige Philosoph, der sich wie eine Schnecke in sein Haus zurückzieht und sich gedanklich in Besinnung und Gebet vertieft. […] Im Gegensatz dazu ist Callot der großmäulige und anzügliche Landsknecht, der auf dem Platz umherstolziert, in der Taverne Krawall schlägt und die Zigeunertöchter unsittlich berührt. […] Der Verfasser dieses Buchs hat die Kunst unter dem Aspekt dieser doppelten Personifizierung betrachtet." Im letzten Absatz schreibt er: „Und sollte man den Verfasser fragen, warum er zu Beginn seines Werks nicht irgendeine hübsche literarische Theorie präsentiert, wäre er zu der Antwort gezwungen, dass auch […] das Kasperle den Haltefaden an seinem Arm vor der neugierigen Menge verbirgt. Er begnügt sich damit, sein Werk wie folgt zu signieren: GASPARD DE LA NUIT." Der Band beinhaltet das Vorwort, eine an Victor Hugo gerichteten Passage, die sechs Bücher „Les fantaisies de Gaspard de la Nuit" mit 51 Gedichten, ein Wort an den Literaturkritiker Charles-Augustin Sainte-Beuve sowie 13 „pièces détachées, extraites du portefeuille de l'auteur". „Ondine" stammt aus dem dritten Gedichtbuch mit dem Titel „La nuit et ses prestiges", während sich „Le gibet" und „Scarbo" in den „pièces détachées" finden.

Ricardo Viñes (1876–1943), ein befreundeter Kommilitone von Ravel am Pariser Konservatorium, hatte den Komponisten mit dem Werk bekannt gemacht. Als der gebürtige Spanier 1887 nach Paris kam, beherrschte er ausschließlich seine eigene Sprache. Innerhalb weniger Jahre aber hatte er nicht nur Französisch gelernt, sondern konnte auch große Teile der französischen Literatur, darunter Baudelaires *Les fleurs du mal*, aus dem Gedächtnis zitieren. Wie durch Viñes' Tagebuch bekannt ist[2], hatte seine Freundschaft zu Ravel neben der musikalischen auch eine literarische Basis. Im August 1892 schrieb Viñes, Ravel habe zwei „sehr düstere" Zeichnungen angefertigt, die durch Geschichten von Edgar Allan Poe inspiriert seien, welche sie gemeinsam in Baudelaires Übersetzung gelesen hätten (*The Maelstrom* und *Manuscript found in a bottle*). Im Oktober 1894 heißt es, dass sie ein halbes Dutzend verbotener Gedichte aus Les fleurs du mal abgeschrieben hätten. Gaspard wird erstmals am 12. November 1895 erwähnt, als Viñes notierte: „[Ravel] sagte mir, dass der Gaspard de la Nuit, den ich in London gekauft habe, sehr selten ist.". Am 25. September 1896 gestattete Viñes Ravel, das Buch mitzunehmen, und erst am 20. Dezember 1897 erhielt er es zurück – mit der Begründung, es habe ganz unten in einer Truhe gelegen! Der nächste Tagebucheintrag zu Gaspard findet sich erst wieder am 25. Oktober 1908, als Viñes mit dem Notenstudium der „Ondine" begonnen hatte. Zwei Tage später spielte er alle drei Sätze Manuel de Falla vor, am 8. November präsentierte er sie außerdem Albert Roussel. Die öffentliche Uraufführung gab Viñes am 9. Januar 1909 im Salle Erard anlässlich eines Konzerts der Société Nationale. Die Presse reagierte im Großen und Ganzen positiv.

Mit seiner Vorliebe für Poe und Baudelaire war Ravel ein durchaus typischer junger Ästhet seiner Zeit. Bertrands Credo vom Kasperle und seinem „vor der neugierigen Menge" verborgenen Haltefaden entsprach ganz seinen eigenen Auffassungen. Doch die Vorstellung, Ravel sei die Deutlichkeit und Präzision in Person gewesen, ja gar ein Dandy oder – in Strawinskys Worten – ein „Schweizer Uhrmacher", ist nur bedingt mit manchen seiner eigenen Äußerungen über *Gaspard* in Einklang zu bringen. Hélène Jourdan-Morhange berichtet von einem Gespräch mit Viñes, in dem der Pianist erklärte, in „Ondine" solle das Thema nicht in den Vordergrund treten, sondern ganz von der umgebenden Atmosphäre aufgenommen werden. Solange diese

Atmosphäre intakt bleibe, würde sich Ravel über eine gelegentliche falsche Note nicht beklagen[3]. „Es macht nichts, wenn man die Rhythmen des Eingangsmotivs nicht genau zählt"[4], soll Ravel dem Pianisten Paul Loyonnet zufolge über „Ondine" gesagt haben.

Es gibt Gründe anzunehmen, dass Ravel Bertrands kontrastierendes Prinzip imitierte, indem er den Mittelsatz so anders wie möglich als die Rahmensätze gestaltete – ein Rembrandt zwischen zwei Callots. Er verlangte, dass „Le gibet" monoton und in einem strikt gleichbleibenden Tempo gespielt werde. Am 24. März 1922 – zu einem Zeitpunkt, als Ravel sich auf die Klavierrollen-Einspielungen für Duo-Art in London vorbereitete – schrieb er in einem Brief an den Kritiker M. D. Calvocoressi: „Vor allem möchte ich Gaspard de la nuit aufnehmen lassen, und Viñes hat diese Stücke – insbesondere ‚Le Gibet' – nie so spielen wollen wie vom Komponisten gedacht. Ich sage bewusst wollen: Ich weiß nicht, ob Sie eine dieser Diskussionen miterlebt haben, bei denen er mir versicherte, dass ‚Le Gibet' dem Publikum auf die Nerven gehen würde, wenn er sich an die Nuancen und Tempi hielte, die ich mir vorgestellt hatte. Davon hat er sich nie abbringen lassen."[5] Zu Henriette Faure sagte Ravel, dass die Glocke nicht lauter als ihre Umgebung sein dürfe: „Diese Glocke steht nicht im Vordergrund, sie ist, sie schlägt unverdrossen."[6]

In den Rahmensätzen bestand Ravel wiederum darauf, dass die Kontraste in der Dynamik beachtet würden[7]. Auch wenn Viñes als Interpret seine Schwächen gehabt haben mag, besteht doch kein Grund, an seiner Aussage zu zweifeln, dass Ravel ausgeprägte Crescendi forderte und dass Pianisten diese im Allgemeinen zu früh ansetzten[8]. Auch der Geist Franz Liszts schwebt über diesen Stücken, und Ravel empfahl Mlle Faure, dass sie an Liszts *Feux follets* arbeiten solle, um ihr schweres Spiel mit den Daumen in „Ondine" zu korrigieren[9]. Er bat sie zudem, den „Scarbo" insgesamt nicht zu laut zu spielen[10], wohl um zu gewährleisten, dass die Höhepunkte den gewünschten schlagenden Effekt erzielen. Weitere Bemerkungen gegenüber anderen Kollegen machen seine Absichten in „Scarbo" noch deutlicher. Henri Gil-Marchex wies er darauf hin, dass man der Phrase in der rechten Hand in Takt 32 die Worte „Quelle horreur!" unterlegen könne[11]; Maurice Delage erklärte er, dass er ein Werk habe komponieren wollen, das schwieriger zu spielen sei als Balakirews Islamey[12]; und zu Vlado Perlemuter sagte er: „Ich wollte eine Karikatur der Romantik zeichnen." Dann aber setzte er flüsternd hinzu: „Vielleicht habe ich es ein wenig übertrieben."[13]

Dass „Le gibet" als Kontrast zu den anderen Sätzen fungiert, wird schließlich auch durch Ravels Wahl der Widmungsträger deutlich. Die zwei Rahmensätze sind jeweils einem Pianisten gewidmet: „Ondine" ist Harold Bauer zugeeignet und „Scarbo" Rudolph Ganz. „Le gibet" jedoch trägt eine Widmung an den Kritiker Jean Marnold, der Ravels Stellung als bedeutender und origineller Künstler verteidigte, als andere Kritiker wie Pierre Lalo ihn als reinen Nachahmer von Debussy abqualifizierten. Nach der Aufführung von *Gaspard de la nuit* war ein solches Plädoyer nicht mehr notwendig.

Zur Editionspraxis

Zusätze des Herausgebers sind mehrheitlich durch eckige Klammern gekennzeichnet: Versetzungszeichen, Noten und Pausen, Taktarten, Dynamik- und Tempovorzeichnungen, Pedalangaben sowie die Hinweise *main droite/main gauche*. Warnungsakzidentien in runden Klammern wurden überall dort aus der Erstausgabe (**E**) übernommen, wo sie hilfreich erschienen. Sämtliche Fingersätze stammen aus Ravels eigenem korrigierten Exemplar von E (**CE**), soweit im Kritischen Bericht nicht anders vermerkt.

Folgende editorische Korrekturen wurden vorgenommen, ohne im Notentext gekennzeichnet oder im Kritischen Bericht aufgeführt zu werden:

Phrasierungsangaben und Bindebögen wurden ergänzt oder korrigiert, um Parallelstellen in Einklang zu bringen. Ebenso wurden in „Le gibet" und „Scarbo" Stakkatopunkte und -striche, Akzente sowie Tenutoangaben nach Maßgabe vergleichbarer Passagen hinzugefügt oder weggelassen. Die in den Quellen mitunter fehlenden Haltebögen zwischen den tiefen B's der wiederholten „Glocken"-Oktaven in „Le gibet" wurden durchgängig ergänzt. In Quelle E sind einige Haltebögen dieser Art falsch platziert, was dazu führen könnte, dass sie als Bindebögen fehlinterpretiert werden. Die vorliegende Ausgabe beseitigt diese Zweifelsfälle durch korrekte Positionierung von Halte- und Bindebögen. Alle unregelmäßigen rhythmischen Gruppierungen sind hier als solche gekennzeichnet; die Quellen enthalten lediglich vereinzelte Triolenangaben.

Roger Nichols, 1991
Übersetzung: Lore Horlamus

---

[1] Jacques Callot (1592–1635) war ein berühmter Kupferstecher. Zu seinen bekanntesten Werken zählen *Les misères de la guerre* und *Les tentations de St Antoine*.

[2] „Le journal inédit de Ricardo Viñes", hg. v. N. Gubisch, *Revue Internationale de Musique Fraçaise* (Juni 1980), S. 155–248.

[3] H. Jourdan-Morhange: *Ravel et nous*, Genf 1945, S. 215 f.

[4] C. Timbrell: „An interview with Paul Loyonnet", in: *Journal of the American Liszt Society*, xix (1986), S. 112–21.

[5] Musikabteilung der Pariser Bibliothèque Nationale, LA Ravel 99.
M. Ravel: *Lettres, écrits, entretiens*, hg. v. A. Orenstein, Paris 1989, S. 196 f.

[6] **FauS** S. 61.

[7] *Ebd.*, S. 65.

[8] *Vgl.* (3).

[9] **FauS** S. 57.

[10] *Ebd.*, S. 65.

[11] Henri Gil-Marchex: „Les Concertos de Ravel", in: *La Revue Musicale* (Dez. 1938), S. 89.

[12] Roland-Manuel: *A la gloire de Ravel*, Paris 1938, S. 54.

[13] **PerS(HJM)** S. 36/35.

Ondine

> . . . . Je croyais entendre
> Une vague harmonie enchanter mon sommeil,
> Et près de moi s'épandre un murmure pareil
> Aux chants entrecoupés d'une voix triste et tendre.
> Ch. Brugnot – *Les deux Génies*

– "Ecoute! – Ecoute! – C'est moi, c'est Ondine qui frôle de ces gouttes d'eau les losanges sonores de ta fenêtre illuminée par les mornes rayons de la lune; et voici, en robe de moire, la dame châtelaine qui contemple à sonbalcon la belle nuit étoilée et le beau lac endormi.

Chaque flot est un ondin qui nage dans le courant, chaque courant est un sentier qui serpente vers mon palais, et mon palais est bati fluide, au fond du lac, dans le triangle du feu, de la terre et de l'air.

Ecoute! – Ecoute! – Mon père bat l'eau coassante d'une branche d'aulne vette, et mes soeurs caressent de leurs bras d'écume les fraîches îles d'herbes, de nénuphars et de glaïeuls, ou se moquent du saule caduc et barbu qui pêche a la ligne."

Sa chanson murmurée, elle me supplia de recevoir son anneau à mon doigt, pour être l'époux d'une Ondine, et de visiter avec elle son palais, pour être le roi des lacs.

Et comme je lui répondais que j'aimais une mortelle, boudeuse et dépitée, elle pleura quelques larmes, poussa un éclat de rire, et s'évanouit en giboulées qui ruisselèrent blanches le long de mes vitraux bleus.

Aloysius Bertrand

> . . . . I thought I heard a vague harmony casting a spell over my slumber, and near me a murmuring break out like the interrupted song of a sad and tender voice.
> Charles Brugnot – *Les deux Génies*

– "Listen! – Listen! – It is I, it is Ondine who brushes with these drops of water the vibrant panes of your window, lit by the melancholy rays of the moon; and here, in a robe of watered silk, is the lady of the castle who, from her balcony, gazes at the beautiful, starry night and the beautiful, sleeping lake.

Each wave is a water-sprite swimming in the current, each current is a path that winds towards my palace, and my palace is built of water, in the depths of the lake, in the triangle of fire, earth and air.

Listen! – Listen! – My father beats the croaking water with a green alder branch, and my sisters caress with their arms of spray the cool islands of grass, of water-lilies and gladioli, or mock the weeping, bearded willow as he dips his fishing-line in the lake."

She finished her murmured song and begged me to put her ring on my finger, to be the husband of a water-nymph, and to come down with her to her palace as king of the lakes.

And when I told her that I was in love with a mortal woman, she began to sulk in annoyance, shed a few tears, gave a burst of laughter, anq vanished in a shower of spray which ran in pale drops down my blue window-panes.

Translation: R. Nichols

> . . . . Mir war, als hörte ich eine verschwommene Harmonie, die mich im Schlaf verzauberte, und ein Flüstern, das ganz in meiner Nähe erklang und dem stockenden Gesang einer traurig sanften Stimme glich.
> Charles Brugnot – *Les deux Génies*

– „Horch! – Horch! – Ich bin es, Undine, die mit diesen Wassertropfen die klingenden Rauten deines vom tristen Schein des Monds erleuchteten Fensters streift; und siehe, hier ist in ihrem schillernden Gewand die Schlossherrin, die auf ihrem Balkon die schöne, sternklare Nacht und den schönen See in seinem Schlaf betrachtet.

Jede Woge ist ein Wassermann, der in der Strömung schwimmt, jede Strömung ist ein Pfad, der sich zu meinem Palast schlängelt, und mein Palast ist ein wässriger Bau auf dem Grund des Sees, im Dreieck zwischen Feuer, Erde und Luft.

Horch! – Horch! – Mein Vater schlägt mit einem grünen Erlenzweig auf das quakende Wasser, und meine Schwestern streicheln mit ihren gischtenen Armen die kühlen Inseln aus Gras, Seerosen und Gladiolen oder verspotten den gebrechlichen, bärtigen Weidenbaum, der da angelt."

Nachdem sie ihr Lied geflüstert hatte, bat sie darum, mir ihren Ring anstecken zu dürfen, damit ich der Gatte einer Undine sei, und mit ihr gemeinsam ihren Palast zu besuchen, damit ich König der Seen sei.

Und als ich ihr entgegnete, dass ich eine Sterbliche liebte, vergoss sie beleidigt und enttäuscht ein paar Tränen, stieß ein schallendes Lachen aus und löste sich in Regenschauer auf, die weiß an meinen blauen Fenstergläsern herunterrannen.

Übersetzung: A. Muus

Gaspard de la nuit
I: Ondine

à Harold Bauer

Maurice Ravel
(1875–1937)

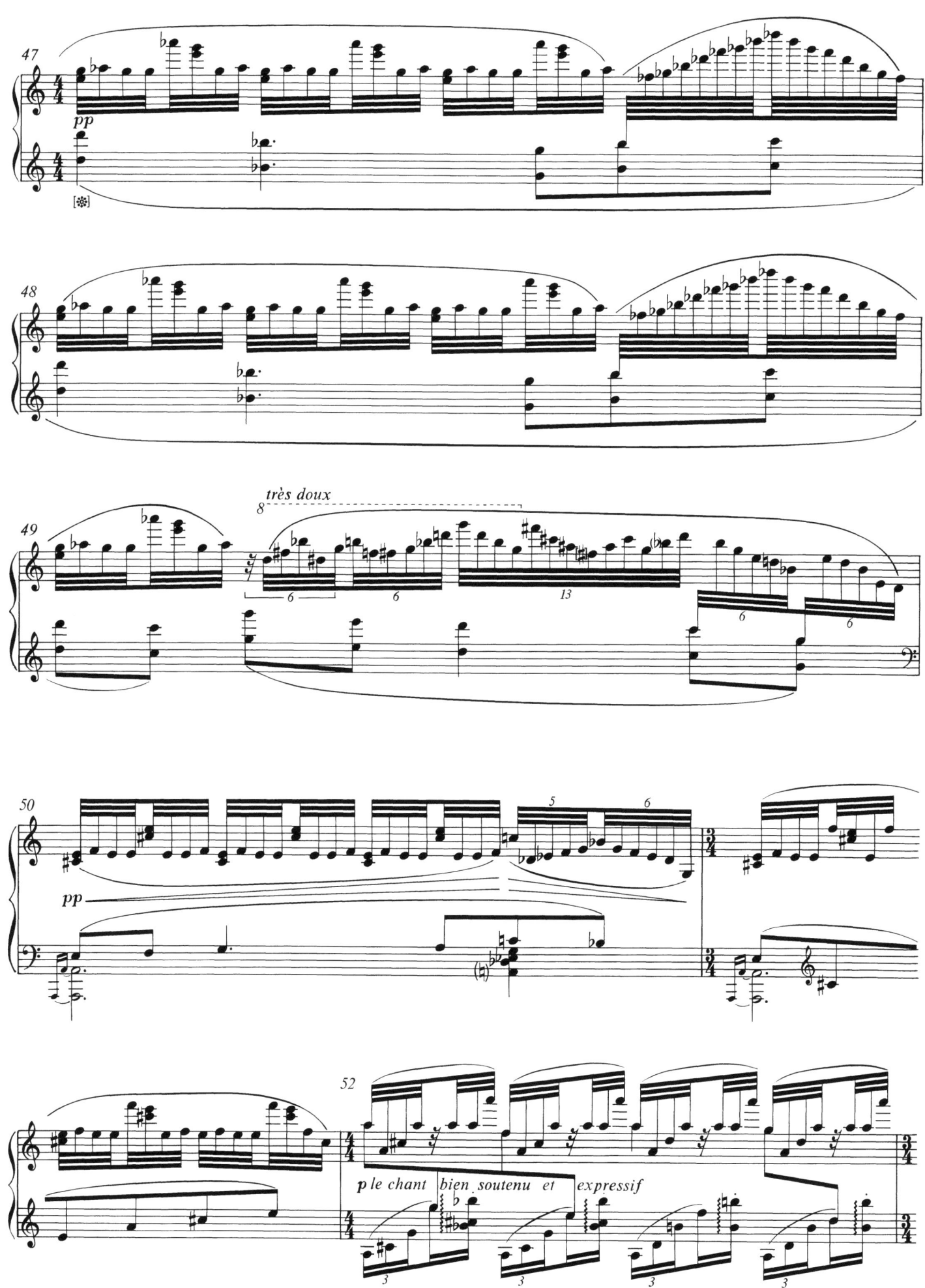

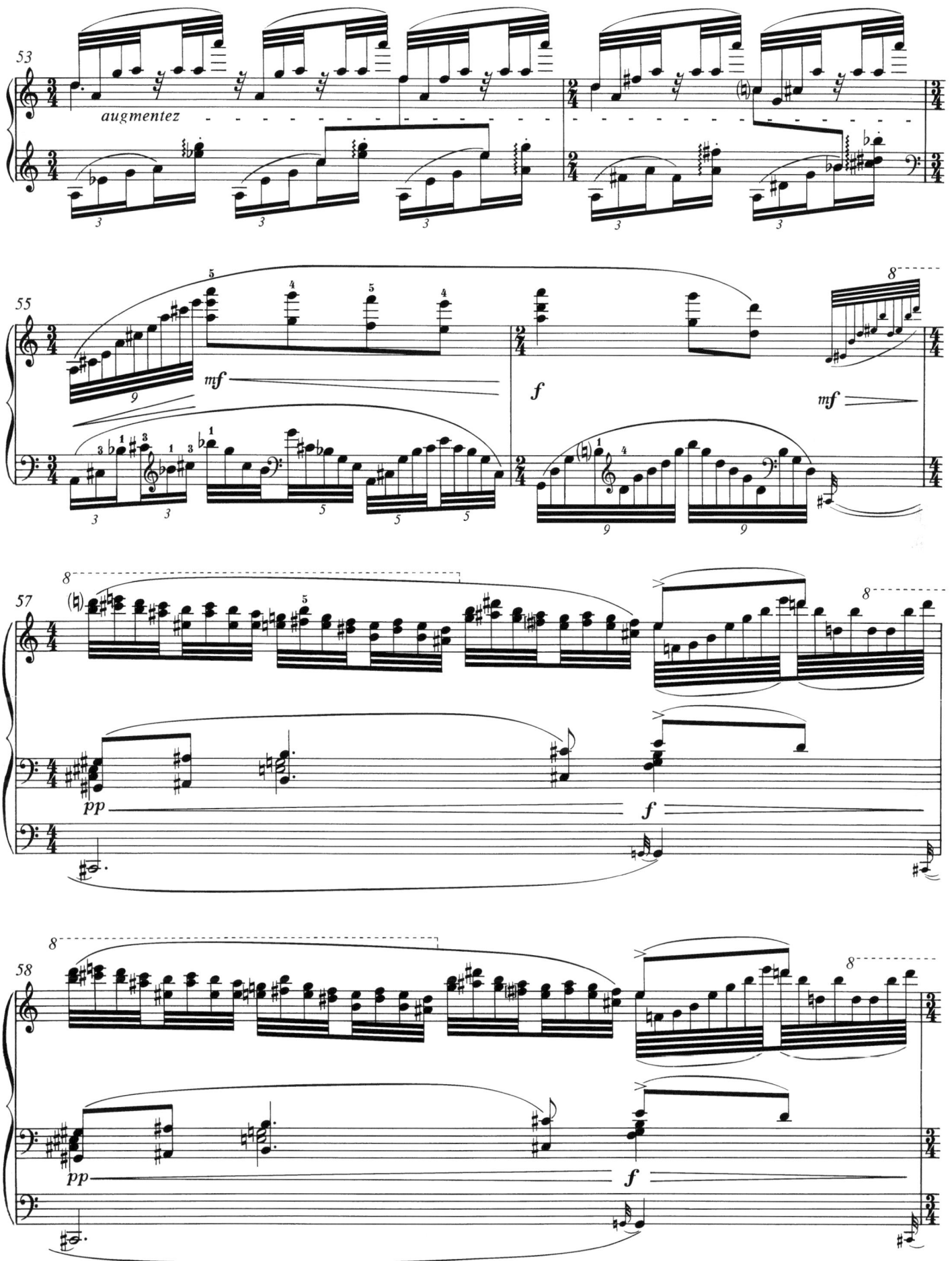

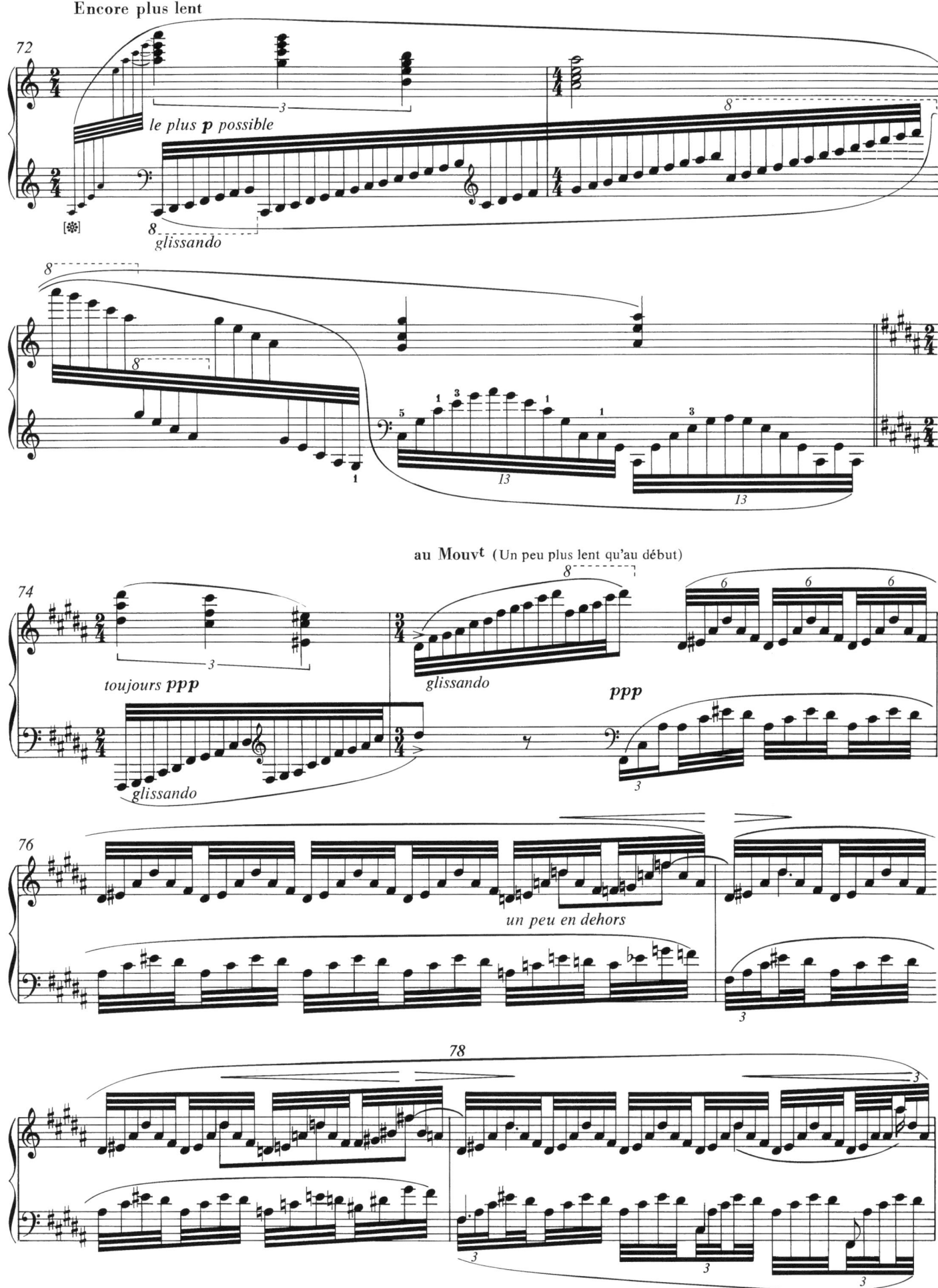

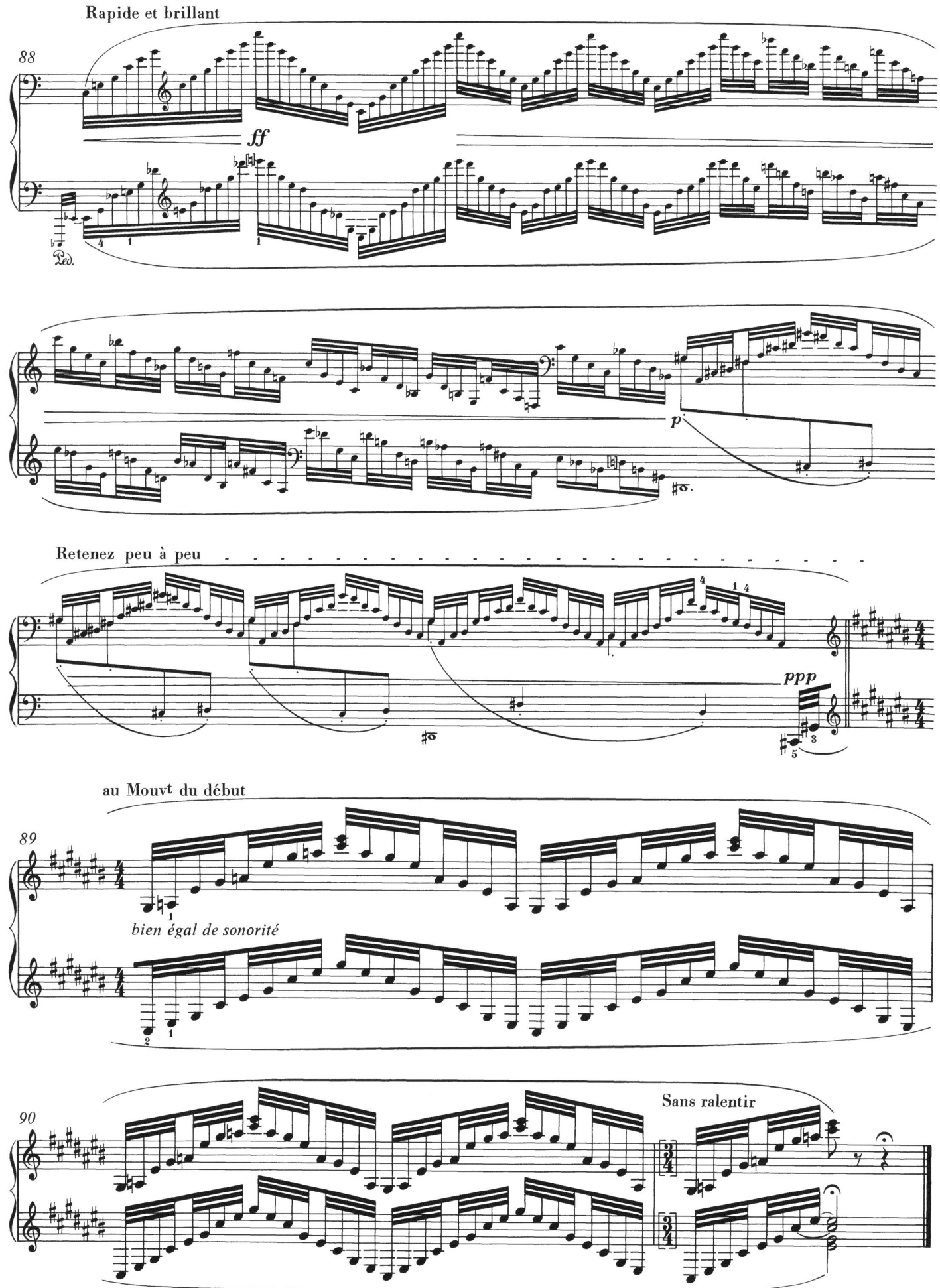

Le gibet

> Que vois-je remuer autour de ce Gibet?
> FAUST

Ah! ce que j'entends, serait-ce la bise nocturne qui glapit, ou le pendu qui pousse un soupir sur la fourche patibulaire?

Serait-ce quelque grillon qui chante tapi dans la mousse et le lierre sterile dont par pitié se chausse le bois?

Serait-ce quelque mouche en chasse sonnant du cor autour de ces oreilles sourdes à la fanfare des hallali?

Serait-ce quelque escarbot qui cueille en son vol inegal un cheveu sanglant à son crâne chauve?

Ou bien serait-ce quelque araignee qui brode une demi-aune de mousseline pour cravate à ce col étranglé?

C'est la cloche qui tinte aux murs d'une ville, sous l'horizon, et la carcasse d'un pendu que rougit le soleil couchant.

Aloysius Bertrand

> What is it I see stirring around that Gibbet?
> FAUST

Ah! What do I hear? Is it the night wind howling, or the hanged man sighing on the gibbet?

Might it be a cricket singing, hidden in the moss and the sterile ivy with which the wood covers itself out of pity?

Might it be a fly hunting and sounding its horn around those ears that are deaf to the slaughterer's triumph?

Might it be a cockchafer plucking, in its halting flight, a bloody hair from its bald pate?

Or might it be a spider, weaving a length of muslin as a scarf for that strangled neck?

It is the bell that sounds from the walls of a town beyond the horizon, and the corpse of a hanged man that glows red in the setting sun.

Translation: R. Nichols

> Was weben die dort um den Rabenstein?
> FAUST

Ach, was höre ich? Sollte es der nächtliche Nordwind sein, der da heult, oder der Gehängte, der am Galgen einen Seufzer ausstößt?

Sollte es eine Grille sein, die da zirpt, während sie in Moos und fruchtlosem Efeu kauert, mit denen das Gebälk aus Mitleid seinen Fuß bedeckt?

Sollte es eine Fliege auf der Jagd sein, die hier ihr Horn bläst, wo der Fanfarenruf der Halalis auf taube Ohren stößt?

Sollte es ein Käfer sein, der auf seinem holprigen Flug ein blutiges Haar vom kahlen Schädel zupft?

Oder sollte es gar eine Spinne sein, die eine halbe Elle feinsten Gewebes als Tuch um diesen abgeschnürten Hals legt?

Es ist die Glocke, die an den Mauern einer Stadt jenseits des Horizonts läutet, und der tote Körper eines Gehängten, den die untergehende Sonne in ein leuchtendes Rot taucht.

Übersetzung: A. Muus

II: Le gibet

à Jean Marnold

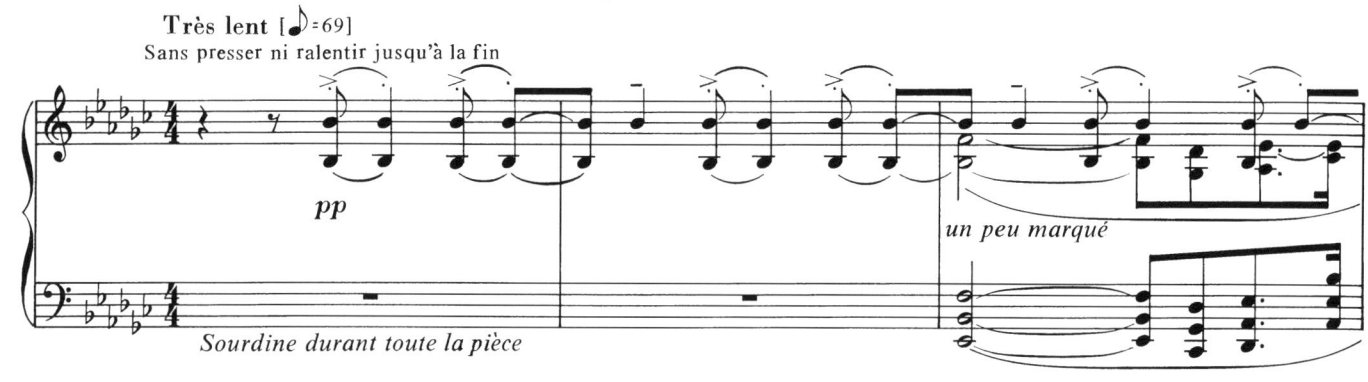

Scarbo

Il regarda sous le lit, dans la cheminée, dans le bahut; – personne. Il ne put comprendre par où il s'était introduit, par ou il s'était évadé.
Hoffmann – *Contes nocturnes*

Oh! que de fois je l'ai entendu et vu, Scarbo, lorsqu'à minuit la lune brille dans' le ciel comme un écu d'argent sur une bannière d'azur semée d'abeilles d'or!

Que de fois j'ai entendu bourdonner son rire dans l'ombre de mon alcove, et grincer son ongle sur la soie des courtines de mon lit!

Que de fois je l'ai vu descendre du plancher, pirouetter sur un pied et rouler par la chambre comme le fuseau tombé de la quenouille d'une sorcière!

Le croyais-je alors évanoui? le nain grandissait entre la lune et moi comme le clocher d'une cathedrale gothique, un grelot d'or en branle à son bonnet pointu!

Mais bientot son corps bleuissait, diaphane comme la eire d'une bougie, son visage blémissait comme la eire d'un lumignon, – et soudain il s'éteignait.

Aloysius Bertrand

He looked under the bed, in the fireplace, in the cupboard – no one. He could not understand where it had got in, or where it had got out.
Hoffmann – *Contes nocturnes*

Oh! how many times have I heard and seen Scarbo, when at midnight the moon shines in the sky like a silver coin on an azure banner dotted with golden bees!

How many times have I heard his laughter buzz in the shadows of my alcove, and his fingernails scratching on the silk curtains round my bed!

How many times have I seen him leap down to the floor, pirouette on one foot and hurtle round the room like the spindle that has fallen from a witch's distaff!

Did I think he had vanished? The dwarf would begin to grow between the moon and me like the steeple of a Gothic cathedral, with a gold bell bobbing on his pointed bonnet!

But soon his body would start to turn blue, as transparent as candle wax, his face would grow pale as the light from a candle-end – and suddenly he would begin to disappear.

Translation: R. Nichols

Er schaute unters Bett, in den Kamin, in den Schrank: niemand. Er konnte nicht verstehen, wodurch er eingetreten war, wodurch er entkommen war.
Hoffmann – *Nachtstücke*

Oh, wie oft habe ich Scarbo gehört und gesehen, wenn der Mond um Mitternacht am Himmel scheint wie ein Silbertaler auf einem tiefblauem Banner, das mit goldenen Bienen übersät ist!

Wie oft habe ich im Dunkel meines Alkovens gehört, wie sein Lachen dröhnt und wie er mit dem Fingernagel an der Seide meiner Bettvorhänge kratzt!

Wie oft habe ich gesehen, wie er sich von der Decke herablässt, auf einem Fuß eine Pirouette vollführt und im Zimmer umherrollt wie eine Spindel, die einer Hexe vom Rocken gefallen ist!

Glaubte ich denn, dass er nun verschwunden sei? Zwischen dem Mond und mir wuchs der Zwerg dann in die Höhe wie der Turm einer gotischen Kathedrale, an dessen Haube eine goldene Schelle schwingt!

Doch stets lief sein Körper schon bald blau an, ließ Licht durch wie das Wachs einer Kerze, sein Gesicht wurde blass wie das Wachs eines Kerzenrests – und plötzlich verlosch er.

Übersetzung: A. Muus

III: Scarbo
à Rudolph Ganz

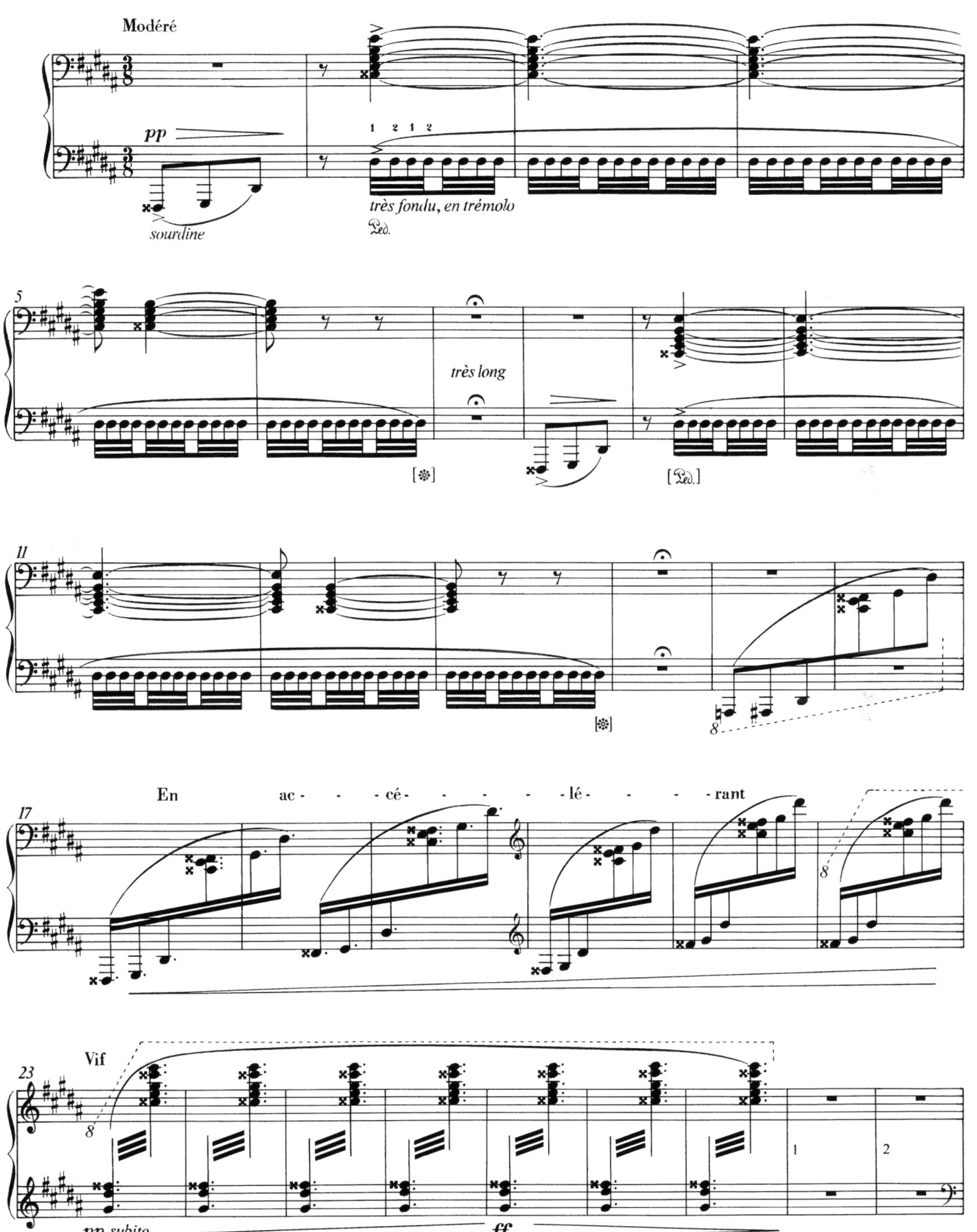

CRITICAL COMMENTARY

Sources: **A** – autograph dated "Mai-Septem 1908", originally held in the archives of MM Durand, now held in the Harry Ransom Humanities Research Center in the University of Texas at Austin
E – first edition published by Durand, deposited at the Bibliothèque Nationale, Paris, on 8 January 1909

For details of all other sources see 'Editorial Method and Sources', p. 3. A table of Source abbreviations appears on p. 4

Ondine

A: no dedication
PerCE: ♩ = 58(60) in Ravel's hand
A: metre C. 4/4 in all other sources
Bars 4-7. **A**, **E**: the pattern established in first 3½ bars is altered from second beat of bar 4 onwards, from xyxxyxxy to xyyxyxxy. **CE**, **PerCE**, **GarCE**: same pattern maintained throughout and in bar 4, RH beat 1, c″♯s of **A** and **E** deleted
Bars 8, 9. **A**, **E**: RH, final quaver, d″♯. **CE**, **PerCE**: d″♯ deleted
Bar 12. It might seem logical to tie final RH a″♮/f″♯ over to beginning of bar 13, by analogy with bars 11–12, but this is not supported by any source. **CasR**, **FévR**, **PerR** all repeat the dyad
Bar 22. **CE**: triplet marking over RH. Does not appear in **A** or **E**
The marking "2 Ped." means that Ravel, as often, has forgotten to indicate where the initial *una corda* should be released. There are no indications in any source
Bar 24. **A**, **E**: RH, final quaver, a″♯. **CE**: a″♮
Bar 27. All sources: RH, initial chord notated as crotchet. *Laisser vibrer* ties added editorially
A: this bar designated as in 3/4. LH chord has remained as dotted minim in all sources. Corrected editorially to semibreve
A, **E**: beat 4, pattern of chords RLLRRLLR. **CE**, **GarCE**: pattern LRRLRLLR maintained
Bar 29. **A**: "Un peu retenu" spaced out over whole bar. Reproduced here as printed in **E**
A, **E**: RH beat 3, g′♯ quaver. **CE**: crotchet
Bar 38. **A**, **E**: LH demisemiquaver 8, g′♯. **CE**: f′♯
Bars 38, 40. **CE**: parenthesis added to RH demisemiquaver 9, g′
Bar 40. **A**: metre C. 4/4 in all other sources
Bar 41. **A**, **E**: beat 3, f″𝄪, LH quaver. **CE**: RH demisemiquaver
Bars 44, 49. **A**: "*très doux*" marking above RH figuration. **E**, **CE**: marked between staves. Here Ravel's indication was probably normalised by the engraver
Bar 46. **A**: RH, final a″♭, octave higher. All other sources as printed here
Bars 47, 48. **A**: RH, final a″♭s of each of first three beats, octave higher. All other sources as printed here
All sources: RH beat 4, notes printed as demisemiquavers. Corrected editorially to hemidemisemiquavers
Bar 52. According to Ravel's instructions, the *una corda* introduced at bar 22 is still in force. Again, it is up to the player to decide when to release it
Bars 53, 54. **CE**: "*augmentez*.....". Does not appear in any other source
Bars 57, 58. All sources: LH beat 2, g♮/e♮ notated as crotchet. Because of held C♯ and crescendo through phrase, this dyad must inevitably sound as a minim; amended editorially. Similarly, bar 60, LH beat 2, f′♮/c′♮
Bar 60. All sources: LH beat 4, it is unclear whether the accent refers to the whole triad or just to c′♯. Applied to c′♯ editorially
CE: diminuendo through final crotchet. Does not appear in any other source
Bar 65. **A**: RH, final quaver, b″♮. c″′♯ in all other sources
Bar 71. **GarCE**: RH, ♮s to d″s and d″′s throughout. The mistake stems from **A**, where Ravel wrote a repeat mark (∕.) in bar 71 instead of the RH figuration, forgetting that ♮s to Ds were supplied by the unrepeated grace notes in bar 70. No ♮s in **E** or **CE**
Bar 72. All sources: "*glissando*" aligned with C. Repositioned editorially
Bar 73. **A**, **E**: RH octava missing. Supplied in **CE**
GarCE: LH, final 2 notes, *octava bassa*. This avoids the slightly awkward double back; on the other hand it interrupts the contrary motion which is the essence of bars 73–74. **CasR** plays *octava bassa*; **FévR**, **PerR** do not
Bar 74. **A**: RH, ♯s to e′ and e″ not in Ravel's hand. **CE**: ♯ to e′ only
Bar 76. RH, *laisser vibrer* tie added editorially to f″♮
Bars 76–78. **PerS(HJM)** 32/31: Ravel wanted the theme in longer notes in RH to be brought out
Bar 77. **A**, **E**: RH beat 2, demisemiquavers 6 and 12, e″♯. **CE**, **PerCE**: f″♯, as on beat 1
RH, *laisser vibrer* tie added editorially to f″♯
Bar 78. All sources: RH beat 3, a″♯ quaver. Corrected editorially
Bar 79. All sources: RH phrase mark is extended to cover final grace notes, even though harmonically they belong with what follows. Amended editorially to conform with bars 56, 59, where grace notes placed before the barline are slurred separately
CE: LH beat 3, G♯ grace note tied to semibreve in bar 80. No tie in any other source
Bar 83. **PerS(HJM)** 32/32: Ravel wanted no rallentando and only a short pause on the rest. (Was this why he marked the pause on LH only?)
Bars 84–87. No pedal indication in any source. **CasR** and **PerRI** clear sound of bar 83 by end of bar, **FévR** and **PerRII** on initial a′♮ of bar 84
Bar 88. **PerS(HJM)** 32/32: LH, Ravel wanted E′♭ and E♭ to be played at full speed and not with undue deliberation
System 2, LH quavers 9 and 10, demisemiquaver beams deleted editorially
PerS(conv): end of system 2, system 3, Ravel suggested using LH thumb on f♯ quavers (finally crotchet), as well as on c♯ and d♯ quavers. All sources notate the g♯–f♯–c♯–d♯ melody line and the bass D♯s in half of true durations; corrected editorially
Bars 88–89. **A**: LH fingerings 5-3-2 only ones in this source for this movement
Bars 89–91. **PerS(conv)**: Ravel suggested that these final bars should be played as though nothing had happened ("comme si rien ne s'était passé")

Le gibet

A: no dedication
PerCE: ♪ = 69 (♪ = 72) not in Ravel's hand. Perlemuter recalls ♪ = 69 as being the tempo Ravel asked for (and this is indeed the basic tempo of **PerR**); he does not now recall whether Ravel authorised the variant ♪ = 72 or not
A: metre C; ♩ = , tempo not indicated. All other sources: 4/4
Bar 4. **CE**: RH, e′♭s tied. No tie in other sources
Bar 7. **CE**: RH, b♭ tied over to bar 8. No tie in other sources
Bar 9. All sources: RH dyad f′♮/b♭ notated as minim. Since there seems no reason to distinguish this bar from bar 5, minim altered editorially to semibreve
CE: RH and LH, both pairs of octave B♭s, lower notes tied. No ties in other sources
Bar 12. **A**: climax of crescendo quite clearly over final semiquaver. Placing in **E** over dotted quaver probably another case of engraver normalising. Uncorrected in **CE**
Bar 17. All sources: *mf* placed between top two staves after first quaver. Since it clearly applies to new phrase and not to repeated B♭s, it has been aligned editorially with minim chords
A: climax of crescendo as in bar 12. Again, uncorrected in **CE**

Bar 24. **A**, **E**, **CE**: LH octave G, a semibreve. **GarCE**: altered to minim. Obviously octave must be released before F♯♮ on beat 4; the temptation to blend it into G♮¹³ on beat 3 should be resisted, as phrase is to be repeated in bar 25

Bar 25. **PerS(conv)**: Ravel asked for last quaver not to be arpeggiated

Bar 31. **CE**: LH, last two ♭bs tied. No tie in other sources

Bar 32. **A**: RH diminuendo begins well before b″♭. **E**: begins above b″♭; unchanged in **CE**. Reading in **A** preferred by analogy with bars 12, 13, 17, 18, where climax focuses on highest note

Bar 35. **E**: climax before final semiquaver. Reading of **A** adopted

Bar 36. All sources: LH beat 4, octave B♭ notated as crotchet

Bar 40. **GarCE**: LH beat 3, ƒ♭s tied. No tie in other sources

Bar 41. RH quaver 1, b′♭ added editorially to join tie from final quaver of bar 40. RH quaver 4, b′♭ and preceding tie deleted editorially by analogy with bar 44

All sources: placing of *mp* indeterminate. Placed editorially under octave F♭

Scarbo

A: no dedication

All sources: no indication of tempo. **CasR**, **FévR**, **PerR** all take "au Mouv^t" at bar 32 at ca. ♩. = 90

Bars 1, 2. **PerS(HJM)** 37/35: Ravel wanted these two bars to sound as though played by a contrabassoon and a drum respectively ("comme un contrebasson", "comme un tambour")
FauS 66: in bar 2, Ravel did not want to hear repeated notes, simply a blurred, velvety atmosphere ("une atmosphère sonore, floue et feutrée")

Bar 15. **A**, **E**, **CE**: as printed here. **GarCE**: F″×, G″♯, D″♯, implying Bösendorfer extension
Ravel gives no indication of where to release *una corda* before its re-employment at bar 65

Bars 23–29, 65–67. All sources: tremolos incorrectly notated in half values

Bar 73. **A**: RH, first chord contains d′♯ and is arpeggiated. **E**, **CE**: d′♯ retained, chord not arpeggiated. **PerCE**: d′♯ deleted in Ravel's hand

Bar 77. **A**: RH semiquaver 3, a′♯. **E**, **CE**: corrected to c″♯

Bars 116–119. **FauS** 63: Ravel wanted each of these upward arpeggios on a diminuendo to die away completely ("tout à fait évanescent")

Bar 119. **A**, **E**, **CE**: no rests. **GarCE**: rests in LH

Bar 142. **A**: RH, final semiquaver, b′♭. **E**: b′♮. **CE**: b′♭ restored

Bars 144–148. **A**, **E**, **CE**: RH, first two semiquaver E♮s are reversed with respect to previous passages (followed in **FévR**, **PerR**). **GarCE** maintains conformity (followed in **CasR**), as in present edition

Bars 151–153. **CE**: phrase mark added

Bar 179, 185, 189. **A**: RH, staccato dot to semiquaver chord. Omitted in **E**, **CE**

Bar 217. **A**: RH, augmentation dot on crotchet. Omitted in all other sources

Bars 223, 226, 243, 246. **A**: climax on semiquaver 2. **E**: climax on semiquaver 3; unchanged in **CE**. Reading in **A** preferred; cf. 'Le gibet', bars 12, 13, 16, 17 etc.
PerS(HJM) 37/36: "He [Ravel] wanted me to make bursts of sound, always very brilliant..." ("Il me demandait les soufflets, toujours très éclatants...")

Bars 229, 230, 250, 251. LH, demisemiquaver beams added editorially

Bars 232–233, 253–254. **E**: faulty alignments between RH and LH; noted in **CE**

Bar 233. **A**: RH, last four notes correctly notated as demisemiquavers (cf. bar 254). **E**, **CE**: semiquavers

Bar 268. **A**, **E**, **CE**: RH, first chord contains d″♯. **PerCE**: d″♯ deleted in Ravel's hand (cf. bar 73)
A, **E**, **CE**: RH, final semiquaver, g″♮. **GarCE**: g″♯, clearly correct

Bar 272. As for bar 268 an octave lower

Bar 298. RH semiquaver 5, g′♮ in **E**. **A**, **CE**: g′♯

Bars 303–305. **A**: phrase mark. Omitted in all other sources

Bar 317. **A**, **GarCE**: LH semiquaver 3, e♮. **E**: e♯, unchanged in **CE**. e♮ clearly correct

Bar 318. **A**: RH, ♮ to e′ not in Ravel's hand, but necessary

Bar 328. All sources: RH rest, 𝄽 Amended editorially

Bar 334. LH, Bösendorfer extension would permit G″♮ for first note

Bars 350, 352. All sources: RH septuplet, hemidemisemiquavers. Amended editorially

Bar 361. **A**: LH, e″♭♭ repeated on semiquaver 4

Bars 367, 368, 370, 371. **PerS(HJM)** 37–38/36: Ravel wanted the marcato octaves in the bass to sound like timpani ("comme des timbales")

Bar 388. All sources: LH tremolo incorrectly notated in half values

Bars 395, 402, 409. Possibly to be played in octaves if Bösendorfer extension available (cf. bar 15), but **GarCE** does not offer this suggestion here

Bar 418. **A**: "Ped.". Not in any other source

Bar 430. **A**: ♩ = ♪ **E**, **CE**: ♩ = ♪ du mouv^t précédent. Either of these relationships can be made to work, but only if "mouvt précédent" is taken to refer to the tempo established at bar 395. From bar 418 some sort of accommodation has to be made to ensure a smooth transition at bars 429–430 (where the tempo relationship is effectively ♩ = ♩. du mouv^t précédent). **CasR**, **FévR**, **PerR** all accelerate markedly from bar 422

Bar 444. **CE**: RH, ♮ added to ƒ″

Bars 445, 446, 447. **CE**: RH beat 1, ♮ added to d′. The omission of this accidental in **E** was due to these bars in **A** being notated on a single staff, with the exception of first note of bar 445

Bars 448–459. **PerS(HJM)** 38/37: Ravel wanted these chromatic seconds played with plenty of pedal

Bars 454–459. All sources: LH arpeggios notated in semiquavers. Amended editorially

Bars 464–467. LH, augmentation dots added editorially to quaver Bs and B♭s

Bars 477, 484, 491. **GarCE**: LH, precautionary ♮ to e

Bar 499. **CE**: RH, final semiquaver, ♯ added to c. Not in any other source

Bar 507. **CE**: RH, final semiquaver, ♯s added to c′ and g. Not in any other source

Bar 510. **CE**: Ravel marks these three pairs of semiquavers to be taken *m.g.*, *m.d.*, *m.g.* Those in bar 518 are marked editorially by analogy

Bar 556. **GarCE**: LH, precautionary ♮ to e. Not in any other source

Bar 578. **A**: LH beat 1, augmentation dots to octave E. Omitted in **E**, **CE**

Bar 614. All sources: penultimate note, D′♯. In the harmonic context of bars 611–614, D′♮ could be taken as more likely. In practice the very low register minimises the force of the distinction

Bar 615. **A**: LH, dotted crotchet. **E**: dot omitted; restored in **CE**

Bar 616. The tempo change could be read more easily as ♩ = ♩. du mouv^t précédent

Bar 626. **PerS(conv)**: B″♮ to be *sec*, unpedalled. **A**: pedal release on B″♮. **E**, **CE**: release before B″♮
FauS 64: Ravel wanted these last two bars to give the impression of a candle being snuffed out (cf. Bertrand poem)
All sources: RH, no treble clef. Added editorially

Bar 627. **A**: LH, crotchet rest; RH, quaver rest. No pause marks. **E**, **CE**: RH and LH, single quaver rests with pause marks
A: signed "Maurice Ravel 5–9 1908"

Roger Nichols
1991